Read Alouds
FOR ALL
Learners

A Comprehensive Plan for

Every Subject, Every Day

GRADES
PreK–8

MOLLY NESS

Foreword By Natalie Wexler

Solution Tree | Press

a division of

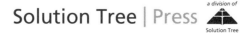

Solution Tree

555 North Morton Street
Bloomington, IN 47404
800.733.6786 (toll free) / 812.336.7700
FAX: 812.336.7790

email: info@SolutionTree.com
SolutionTree.com

Visit **go.SolutionTree.com/literacy** to download the free reproducibles in this book.

Printed in the United States of America

Library of Congress Cataloging-in-Publication Data

Names: Ness, Molly, author.
Title: Read alouds for all learners : a comprehensive plan for every
    subject, every day, grades PreK-8 / Molly Ness.
Description: Bloomington, IN : Solution Tree Press, [2023] | Includes
    bibliographical references and index.
Identifiers: LCCN 2023020277 (print) | LCCN 2023020278 (ebook) | ISBN
    9781958590034 (paperback) | ISBN 9781958590041 (ebook)
Subjects: LCSH: Oral reading. | Reading (Elementary) | Reading (Middle
    school)
Classification: LCC LB1573.5 .N46 2023 (print) | LCC LB1573.5 (ebook) |
    DDC 372.45/2--dc23/eng/20230426
LC record available at https://lccn.loc.gov/2023020277
LC ebook record available at https://lccn.loc.gov/2023020278

Solution Tree
Jeffrey C. Jones, CEO
Edmund M. Ackerman, President

Solution Tree Press
President and Publisher: Douglas M. Rife
Associate Publishers: Kendra Slayton and Todd Brakke
Editorial Director: Laurel Hecker
Art Director: Rian Anderson
Copy Chief: Jessi Finn
Production Editor: Kate St. Ives
Copy Editor: Evie Madsen
Proofreader: Elijah Oates
Text and Cover Designer: Laura Cox
Acquisitions Editor: Hilary Goff
Assistant Acquisitions Editor: Elijah Oates
Content Development Specialist: Amy Rubenstein
Associate Editor: Sarah Ludwig
Editorial Assistant: Anne Marie Watkins

Acknowledgments

Many thanks go to Sarah Jubar (for her vision), the Solution Tree team (for its attention to detail), my colleagues from Learning Ally (for their fierce commitment to literacy equity and for their support), the board and staff of the International Literacy Association (for its knowledge and perspective), my Coalition for Literacy Equity network (for its determination to ensure *all* children have access to books and reading culture), and to my reading research friends (for geeking out with me and sharing the passion for best practices).

My love and gratitude go to friends and family—especially my Adelaide and Roosevelt friends (for the food, entertainment, and childcare), to my fellow boat-rockers from pRYEde (for friendship and advocacy), and to the Stateline parents (for carpools and camaraderie).

And to Callie, for reminding me of what really matters.

> If we are not helping students to become confident, habitual readers, I don't know what business we are in.
>
> —Carol Jago

Solution Tree Press would like to thank the following reviewers:

Lindsey Bingley
Literacy and Numeracy Lead
Foothills Academy
Calgary, Alberta, Canada

Courtney Burdick
Apprenticeship Mentor Teacher
Spradling Elementary—
   Fort Smith Public Schools
Fort Smith, Arkansas

Jenna Fanshier
Principal
Marion Elementary School
Marion, Kansas

Colleen Fleming
Literacy Specialist
Calgary, Alberta, Canada

Kelli Fuller
Instructional Facilitator
Howard Perrin Elementary School
Benton, Arkansas

Visit **go.SolutionTree.com/literacy** to download the free reproducibles in this book.

Table of Contents

Reproducibles are in italics.

About the Author

Molly Ness, PhD, is a former classroom teacher, reading researcher, and teacher educator. She spent sixteen years as an associate professor of childhood education at Fordham University, where she taught literacy methods coursework and doctoral courses in language, literacy, and learning. Her research focuses on reading comprehension, teachers' instructional decisions, and dyslexia. In 2022, Molly joined the nonprofit, Learning Ally (previously Recording for the Blind & Dyslexic; https://learningally.org) as Vice President of Academic Content.

Molly serves on the board of directors for the International Literacy Association and elementary advisory panel for Penguin Random House. She began her career as a middle school teacher in Oakland, California, and later worked as a diagnostic reading clinician. She is a staff member of The Windward Institute, an independent day school focused on teaching grades 1–9 students with language-based learning disabilities. Her publications have appeared in *Pediatrics*, *The Reading Teacher*, *Reading and Writing*, *Journal of Research in Childhood Education*, and *Psychology Today*. In 2019, Molly began her *End Book Deserts* podcast (https://endbookdeserts.com) to bring attention to the issue of book access and equity. Committed to literacy as an issue of social justice, Molly cofounded the Coalition for Literacy Equity (https://litequity.com) in 2022. As the author of four books, she frequently speaks and presents at regional and national conferences.

Molly graduated Phi Beta Kappa from Johns Hopkins University. She earned a master's in English education and a doctorate in reading education from the University of Virginia. When not reading and writing about literacy, Molly is paddleboarding off the coast of Maine, shuttling her daughter to ice hockey practice, wandering the aisles of farmers' markets and independent bookstores, or hiking with her goofy goldendoodle.

To learn more about Molly's work, visit her website (https://drmollyness.com) or follow @drmollyness on Twitter.

To book Molly Ness for professional development, contact pd@SolutionTree.com.

Foreword

By Natalie Wexler

Years ago, when I was touring a middle school serving students from lower-income families, I saw a teacher reading aloud from *The Autobiography of Malcolm X* while her students followed along with their own copies. You could have heard a pin drop. But I remember thinking: What a waste of time! Shouldn't these seventh or eighth graders be reading the book themselves?

I now realize how wrong I was. As Molly Ness explains so clearly in *Read Alouds for All Learners: A Comprehensive Plan for Every Subject, Every Day, Grades PreK–8*, reading aloud isn't just a way to amuse or engage young children before they've learned to decode. It's a vital building block of literacy teachers too often overlook.

Consider a study in England with 365 students in the equivalent of seventh grade. The teachers of these students read aloud two challenging novels over the course of twelve weeks. After being read to during that twelve-week period, a standardized test measured that all students had made significant gains in reading comprehension. On average, the readers who were at grade level or higher made nine months' worth of progress. But the poorer readers—those at least a year behind where they should have been—improved the most, making an average of sixteen months of progress[1] (Westbrook, Sutherland, Oakhill, & Sullivan, 2019). A similar unpublished study with elementary students had similar results—and in some cases even more dramatic.[2]

Why might listening to books being read aloud have such a powerful effect? One reason is before students are fluent independent readers, listening to an expert reader is the most efficient way to build the knowledge and vocabulary crucial to reading comprehension. Students' listening comprehension exceeds their reading comprehension through about

---

1   Some of the twenty teachers in the study had students do the reading aloud themselves in round-robin fashion, but qualitative evidence indicated that practice "supported neither fluency nor comprehension."

2   For a video interview on that study, see https://films.myattandco.com/programs/just-reading-primary-project?categoryId=64012&permalink=just-reading-primary-project-part-1

age thirteen, on average. That means students can take in more sophisticated concepts and vocabulary through listening than through their own reading.

One way of explaining this is to look to something called *cognitive load theory*, which many studies have empirically tested. Basically, the theory says that *working memory*—the aspect of consciousness that takes in and makes sense of new information—is seriously limited. Working memory can only juggle perhaps four or five items for twenty to thirty seconds before becoming overwhelmed. That burden is called *cognitive load*.

When students are still learning to read fluently, the act of reading itself imposes a heavy cognitive load (in addition to the burden of understanding whatever content they're trying to comprehend). Students may have to think about how to sound out unfamiliar words or where to place the emphasis in a sentence. But if an expert reader is doing that work for them—and reading at an appropriate pace, with appropriate expression—students have more space in working memory to absorb the content. That's why it's important to read aloud more complex texts to students than those they can read themselves. These read alouds build up a warehouse of new information and vocabulary students will draw on for years to come.

This new information and vocabulary can then boost students' own reading comprehension. That's because the way around the constraints of working memory is through long-term memory, which is potentially infinite. If readers can simply withdraw relevant information from long-term memory—like vocabulary relating to the topic of the text they're reading—they don't have to juggle that information in working memory. That opens up more cognitive capacity for understanding new information in the text. (Please note, however, that reading aloud by itself won't enable most students to decode words; for that, they'll need systematic phonics instruction.)

But simply listening to a read aloud is generally not enough to get information to stick in long-term memory. For that to happen, educators must attach some meaning to the information, and one good way of doing that is to talk about it, perhaps by explaining it to another person. That's why it's important to engage students in discussion about a text they've just listened to, and have them articulate the concepts and use the vocabulary they've heard.

Sometimes it may be enough to just pause when you sense students have lost the thread of a read aloud and ask where they stopped understanding, like some teachers in the study (Westbrook et al., 2019). However, generally speaking, it's crucial for teachers to read a text ahead of time and plan questions to ask. That's something many teachers don't do, perhaps because they haven't gotten good information about how to do it or why it's important. For teachers eager to learn how to make read alouds work well, this book will provide valuable guidance.

Ideally, teachers will read aloud a series of texts on the same topic to the whole class, using a content-rich curriculum. If students hear the same concepts and vocabulary repeatedly in different contexts, that information is more likely to stick in long-term memory. Once students have built knowledge of a topic through listening and discussion, you may well find they can read about that topic at a higher level.

Several studies suggest evidence that listening to and discussing a topic build knowledge, including an iconic study that had junior high school students read a passage describing a baseball game and then answer comprehension questions. In this study, the students were divided into four groups, depending on how well they'd scored on a standardized reading test and how much they knew about baseball. Researchers found that the students the test identified as "poor readers" who were also baseball experts outperformed the "good readers" who didn't know much about the sport (Recht & Leslie 1988). In other words, when those "poor readers" were able to draw on knowledge they acquired—most likely not through their own reading but through a combination of listening and discussion, along with watching and perhaps playing baseball—they suddenly turned into "good readers."

Eventually, as students acquire knowledge of more topics, their general academic vocabulary will grow to the point where they should be able to read and understand any grade-level text. The more general academic knowledge a person has, the better the person's general reading comprehension (Willingham, 2012). Several studies with young students show curricula incorporating content-rich read alouds have statistically significant effects on general reading comprehension (Bocala, McMaken, & Melchior, 2019; Cabell & Hwang 2020; Gray, Sirinides, Fink, & Bowden, 2022; Kim, Rich, & Scherer, 2022).

But academic vocabulary isn't the only valuable knowledge students can acquire through read alouds. They can also become familiar with the complex syntax of written language, which is almost always more complex than spoken language. Sentences in text tend to be longer, with constructions like subordinate clauses and passive voice. Lack of familiarity with these kinds of syntaxes can be a serious barrier to comprehension, even if students have become fluent decoders (Scott & Balthazar, 2013).

Reading aloud can also build a classroom community. The standard approach to reading instruction is to match students to texts at their individual reading levels, meaning that students in the same class are all reading different books, with the less-able readers reading much simpler texts. Not only does this practice deprive those students of what they need—*access to more complex knowledge and vocabulary*—it also divides the class into de facto tracks. When all students in a class have access to the same content through read alouds and discussion, the weaker readers—the students with Individualized Education Programs (IEPs), those still learning English, and so on—can be the ones who blossom the most. Teachers who have switched to this approach have told me it's often those students who make the most insightful contributions to class discussions. That changes the teachers' own expectations, boosts those students' confidence and sense of belonging, and transforms the way their peers see them.

The bottom line is that reading aloud has huge potential benefits for all students, and especially for those less able to acquire academic knowledge and vocabulary at home. But it's not simply good for students; they also love it when it's done well. During that study in England, students who had been unmotivated readers were suddenly eager to hear the next chapter (Westbrook et al., 2019). I've been in classrooms where students groaned when the allotted time for the read aloud was over because they wanted the teacher to keep going!

Years after I was in that middle school classroom where the teacher was reading aloud *The Autobiography of Malcolm X*, I found myself in another middle school classroom—this one in a working-class neighborhood in London—where the teacher was reading aloud from *Jane Eyre*. Again, you could have heard a pin drop, even though the nineteenth-century boarding school being described was worlds away from the environment these students knew.

This time, I knew better than to dismiss the read aloud as a waste of time. And sure enough, I was told later that this after-school read aloud class, reserved for the school's most challenged readers, seemed to be enormously successful in getting those students caught up to where they needed to be.

With the guidance in Molly Ness's *Read Alouds for All Learners: A Comprehensive Plan for Every Subject, Every Day, Grades PreK–8*, any teacher can unlock the power of read alouds and, along with thoughtful questions and discussions, help all students achieve at higher levels and reach their full potential.

Natalie Wexler is an education writer and author of *The Knowledge Gap: The Hidden Cause of America's Broken Education System—And How to Fix It* (Avery, 2019). She is co-author, with Judith C. Hochman, of *The Writing Revolution: A Guide to Advancing Thinking Through Writing in All Subjects and Grades* (Jossey-Bass, 2017). Her essays and articles have appeared in such publications as *The New York Times*, *The Washington Post*, and *The American Scholar*. Natalie speaks widely on education and has appeared on television and radio shows, including NPR's *On Point* and *1A*. She holds a bachelor's degree from Harvard University, a master's degree in history from the University of Sussex, and a law degree from the University of Pennsylvania.

References and Resources

Bocala, C., McMaken, J., & Melchior, K. (2019). *Evaluating the use of EL education's K–2 language arts curriculum*. Accessed at https://files.eleducation.org/web/downloads/Evaluating-the-Use-of-EL-Education's-K-2-Language-Arts-Curriculum-Feb-2021.pdf on June 19, 2023.

Cabell, S. Q., & Hwang, H. (2020). Building content knowledge to boost comprehension in the primary grades. *Reading Research Quarterly*, *55*(S1), S97–S107. https://doi.org/10.1002/rrq.338

Gray, A. M., Sirinides, P. M., Fink, R. E., & Bowden, A. B. (2022) Integrating literacy and science instruction in kindergarten: Results from the efficacy study of *Zoology One*. *Journal of Research on Educational Effectiveness*, *15*(1), 1–27. https://doi.org/10.1080/19345747.2021.1938313

Kim, J. S., Rich, P., & Scherer, E. (2022, July). *Long-term effects of a sustained content literacy intervention on third graders' reading comprehension outcomes* (Ed Working Paper: 22–600). Accessed at https://edworkingpapers.com/ai22-600 on May 2, 2023.

Recht, D. R., & Leslie, L. (1988). Effect of prior knowledge on good and poor readers' memory of text. *Journal of Educational Psychology*, *80*(1), 16–20.

Scott, C. M., & Balthazar, C. (2013). The role of complex sentence knowledge in children with reading and writing difficulties. *Perspectives on Language and Literacy*, *39*(3), 18–30.

Westbrook, J., Sutherland, J., Oakhill, J., & Sullivan, S. (2019). 'Just reading': The impact of a faster pace of reading narratives on the comprehension of poorer adolescent readers in English classrooms. *Literacy*, *53*(2), 60–68.

Willingham, D. (2012, March 7). *School time, knowledge, and reading comprehension* [Blog post]. Accessed at www.danielwillingham.com/daniel-willingham-science-and-education-blog/school-time-knowledge-and-reading-comprehension on May 2, 2023.

Introduction

Let me begin with a scene from the classic 1977 children's book by Harry Allard, *Miss Nelson Is Missing!* In this story, the sweet Miss Nelson gently attempts to guide her unruly, disruptive students into focused study. However, the students of room 207 live up to their reputation as the "worst-behaved class in the whole school," and ignore their lessons and Miss Nelson (p. 3). They send spitballs whizzing through the air, make rude faces, and whisper and giggle through story time. In her soft-spoken voice, Miss Nelson reminds the students to settle down. When she can no longer tolerate their antics, she disappears with the triumphant declaration, "Something will have to be done!" (p. 7). The next day, the class meets Miss Swamp, a no-nonsense substitute teacher. Ever the disciplinarian, Miss Swamp sets the students to work. She punishes with an authoritarian, "We'll have no story hour today!" (p. 14). And with that declaration, the children lose out on one of their favorite parts of the day—a teacher-led read aloud.

I love this picture book for a few reasons. It evokes a memory of my beloved teacher— Miss Andrews—who welcomed me to first grade with this book. As a former classroom teacher myself, I used this book as a mentor text to model inference as a reading strategy; the author and illustrator cleverly plant clues throughout the text to help savvy readers infer that Miss Swamp is actually a disguised Miss Nelson. I've helped countless readers of all ages unpack these clues to decipher Miss Swamp's true identity. And the book's underlying theme is gratitude and appreciation for the kind individuals in our lives— like teachers.

That being said, my least favorite part of the book is what Miss Swamp does to punish her class: eliminate the read aloud. As a parent and former teacher, babysitter, coach, and camp counselor, I've doled out my fair share of punishments. I've had students write letters of apology to those they've wronged. I've disallowed campers to attend the coveted s'mores night. As a coach, I've added extra lap running as a punishment. As a parent, I've canceled play dates, revoked electronic privileges, and even threatened the ubiquitous "Don't make me pull this car over!" These punishments have met with varying levels of success, but here's one hill I'm willing to die on: I will never deny students the essential experience of a daily read aloud.

Let me say that again, loud and proud: *the read aloud is necessary for every student, every day—regardless of age, grade level, or language background.* A read aloud is not an add-on activity, one to simply do when there's extra time. In school, a read aloud is not a waste of instructional time, nor is it purely entertainment (McCaffrey & Hisrich, 2017). A read aloud is not something that "would be nice to do, if there were time." A read aloud is not a luxury. A read aloud is a *must do*, a *will do*, and always a *get to do*. It is an opportunity to nurture students at a multifaceted level—emotionally, intellectually, linguistically, and developmentally. Simply put, read alouds are essential—for all children and all students, across all grade levels, and across all subject areas. I embrace the daily read aloud as the cornerstone of literacy instruction.

This book is for those who develop and conduct read alouds with elementary and middle school students (that is, PreK–8 teachers and, in many cases, curriculum designers, literacy coaches, and school leaders). I choose to focus on this grade range because these are the grades in which teachers typically already incorporate read alouds to some extent and, therefore, their students may gain the most from these teachers further fine-tuning and implementing read alouds. Though much has been written to help teachers select books to read aloud (Ross, 2017) and understand teachers' text selections (Smith, Young, & Yatzeck, 2022), my specific aim with this book is to provide intentional directions on how to plan and implement the read aloud to support young learners in that multifaceted way I spoke of—emotionally, intellectually, linguistically, and developmentally. As instructors of preservice teachers Megan McCaffrey and Katy E. Hisrich (2017) purport, "Powerful read alouds do not simply happen. Planning is an essential practice for quality instruction and read alouds are no exception" (p. 99). Unfortunately, since teachers often dismiss read alouds as something extra or nice to do if there is time in the school day, essential planning is often not part of their read aloud practice. Researchers Douglas Fisher, James Flood, Diane Lapp, and Nancy Frey (2004) note:

> While the research is quite clear on the importance of instructing through read-alouds, studies are limited on addressing the question of how to conduct an effective read-aloud. . . . In Jim Trelease's handbooks on read alouds (e.g., 1989), he eloquently explained the importance of read-alouds but stopped short of providing an instructional model. Thus, the exact components of a read-aloud have been difficult to discern. (p. 9)

I attempt to fill the void by articulating the components of read alouds and their importance, and by offering a clear instructional plan for designing and carrying out a successful read aloud across grade levels and subject areas. Along the way, I share fascinating interdisciplinary research—from the fields of neuroscience, medicine, psychology, and education—highlighting the relevance and benefits of read alouds. I explore the vast instructional benefits of read alouds for promoting a love of literature, fostering social interactions, and igniting a passion for lifelong reading habits. I leverage my experience as a former middle school teacher, reading clinician, university professor, and teacher educator to offer tools, strategies, and guidance to readers so they may finish this book feeling confident they have the ability to either deepen the read alouds they already do in their classes or begin the practice of reading aloud with their students for rich, engaged learning. In this introduction, I prepare readers for this work by defining what a read aloud is and establishing its benefits, particularly the social-emotional, academic, and motivational benefits. I touch on the current state of read alouds in many classrooms, and I go on to discuss the need for read alouds in everyday classroom instruction. Last, I explain how to use this book, what it contains, and how you, the reader, may apply it in your read alouds in PreK–8 classrooms.

The Definition of a Read Aloud

Educators all have different ideas of what the read aloud looks like: early childhood educators may see the read aloud as a rocking chair in front of a carpet full of eager listeners, whereas middle school teachers might read aloud in short bursts from primary sources in a unit on the Civil War. A key message in this book is that there is no "right" or "wrong" way to read aloud. But before I dig into that, it's useful to clarify the terms *read aloud* and *interactive read aloud*.

The International Literacy Association's (n.d.) glossary defines the *read aloud* as:

> The practice of a teacher or designated reader orally reading a text with large or small groups. Pictures or text may be shared visually with the students whose primary role is to listen and view the illustrations. The intent is to model proficient reading and language, promote conversation, motivate, and extend comprehension and conceptual understandings.

Assistant professor of early childhood education at Georgia State University, Laura May (2011) explains that in an *interactive read aloud*, a reader uses voice, facial expressions, and gestures to interpret the text and guide students' responses.

I define a *read aloud* as a shared literacy experience engaging children and adults in conversation and engagement around a high-quality text. I use the terms *read aloud* and *interactive read aloud* interchangeably because of the interaction and give-and-take of ideas and naturally occurring conversation all read alouds should include. The following points summarize some of the key components of an interactive classroom read aloud.

- Interaction and involvement of students; a give-and-take of language and conversation (Blewitt & Langan, 2016)

- Teachers play multiple roles (fellow wonderers, speculators, and interpreters; Sipe, 2008)

- Joyful and engaging experience for everyone involved (Vlach, Lentz, & Muhammad, 2023)

- Deliberate inclusion of high-quality, reflective text of any form and format

- An invitation from the teacher to talk about the text before, during, and after reading (Beck & McKeown, 2001)

- Frequent verbal exchanges and co-construction of meaning among teachers and students through open-ended dialogue (Wiseman, 2011)

Another important note: in most cases, I refer to the read aloud as an adult-facilitated experience, where the adult is the one doing the reading. However, there are also exciting possibilities of developmental advances when students are the ones delivering read alouds—in school to fellow students, outside school to other students or siblings, to elderly volunteers, or even to inanimate objects like stuffed animals. A study shows when second graders identified as struggling readers read aloud to registered therapy dogs for thirty minutes a week (in a six-week intervention program), the students' attitudes toward reading significantly improved (Linder, Mueller, Gibbs, Alper, & Freeman, 2018). Because the intent of this book is to help teachers plan their read alouds, I focus largely on teacher-provided read alouds. Additional titles—listed in the appendices—focus on the benefits of reading aloud outside school.

The Benefits of Read Alouds

Read alouds are timeless. Learners never outgrow the undeniably rich benefits of read alouds. You'll see in the following body of literature—much of it from seminal research—the benefits of read alouds for primary, elementary, and secondary students are great and varied.

- Develop students' identities as readers (Wiseman, 2012).

- Serve as a model for students' independent writing (Graham, Bollinger, Booth Olson, D'Aoust, MacArthur, McCutchen et al., 2012), and increase students' content knowledge (Strachan, 2015).

- Build students' vocabulary and expressive, receptive, and written communications (Baker, Mogna, Rodriguez, Farmer, & Yovanoff; 2016; Dowdall, Melendez-Torres, Murray, Gardner, Hartford, & Cooper, 2020).

- Promote attitudes toward reading, including understandings of the purpose of reading (Price, van Kleeck, & Huberty, 2009), and increase likelihood to engage in independent reading (Ledger & Merga, 2018).

- Improve longitudinal academic achievement, including larger vocabularies and more advanced comprehension skills (Mol & Bus, 2011).

- Promote foundational literacy skills, including phonological awareness (Mol & Bus, 2011; Zucker, Ward, & Justice, 2009) and print concepts, and comprehension (Duke, Ward, & Pearson, 2021; Santoro, Baker, Fien, Smith, & Chard, 2016).

- Build positive impact on the language skills of young students with developmental disabilities or delays (Towson, Akemoglu, Watkins, & Zeng, 2021).

- Develop students' content knowledge and vocabulary in content-area classrooms (Dwyer & Martin-Chang, 2023), such as science, even in virtual instruction (Gibbs & Reed, 2023).

- Foster students' higher-order-thinking skills (Lennox, 2013).

With each emerging study, I am dazzled by the knowledge that reading aloud—a simple, low-cost practice—improves human beings academically, emotionally, even physically.

Even the neuroscience behind read alouds is impressive. For example, when preschool-aged children listen to an adult read, they undergo observable (through functional MRI scans) cognitive stimulation and healthy brain development. In fact, researchers at Cincinnati Children's Hospital Medical Center explain that shared readings "turbocharge the development of foundational emergent literacy skills in preschool children" (Hutton, Phelan, Horowitz-Kraus, Dudley, Altaye, DeWitt et al., 2017, p. 9). More specifically, researchers can pinpoint the role of the brain's cerebellum, which has the largest number of neurons in the central nervous system. The *cerebellum* plays an important role in higher-level cognitive skills, like language processing and executive function. As John S. Hutton, a pediatrician in the Cincinnati Children's Hospital Division of General & Community Pediatrics and director of the Reading and Literacy Discovery Center, and colleagues' (2017) research demonstrates when engaging in read alouds, preschool students use the cerebellar associate areas, resulting in enhanced comprehension and language processing. In addition, reading aloud promotes the rapid development of neural and auditory systems in children this age, as well as the development of language and attention.

Another astounding article shows when hospitalized children listen to stories, their pain levels decrease, as demonstrated through higher levels of *oxytocin*—a neurotransmitter associated with pleasure—and lower levels of *cortisol*—a neurotransmitter associated with stress (Brockington, Moreira, Buso, da Silva, Altszyler, Fischer et al., 2021). Interviews with hospitalized children also reveal a lessening of anxiety, a growing sensation of calm, and an increase of trusting behavior. This team of scientists use these groundbreaking findings to explain the power of listening to stories:

> Children, albeit momentarily, are transported to another possible world during storytelling sessions. That world, distant from the anxiety-provoking hospital environment and the tedious, if not utterly aversive, ICU setting, can elicit positive physiological and psychological changes. (Brockington et al., 2021, p. 5)

Finally, reading aloud offers health benefits to medically fragile babies. In a 2019 study at the NICU at the University of Virginia, mothers read to their newborn babies for at least thirty minutes, three times per week, at a decibel level and duration appropriate to the baby's medical condition; the most medically fragile babies received whisper reading for five minute sessions, while more robust babies—those soon to be discharged—were read to at regular voice levels for longer durations (Campbell, 2019). Babies' heart rates and oxygen saturation levels were assessed thirty minutes prior to each reading, during the reading, and thirty minutes after the reading. Ready for the *wow factor*? Babies' heart rates slowed—indicating decreased stress and increased relaxation—and infants' blood oxygen rates increased to healthier levels. Better yet, these improved rates were noted even after the read aloud ended! Additionally, mothers reported that reading aloud to their newborns improved their ability to bond with their infant, made them more likely to continue read alouds at home, and decreased their feelings of postpartum depression (Campbell, 2019).

While the wide-ranging benefits of the shared read aloud are amazing, since the majority of ideas I present in this book pertain to read alouds in school, I focus most specifically on three categories of benefits most germane to education: (1) social-emotional, (2) cognitive and academic, and (3) motivational.

The Social-Emotional Benefits of Read Alouds

Read alouds support and enhance students' social-emotional development. As they encounter differing perspectives and characters in read alouds, students develop their ability to resolve conflict and strengthen interpersonal skills (McTigue, Douglass, Wright, Hodges, & Franks, 2015). In their early childhood classrooms, coauthors Shelby Britt, Julia Wilkins, Jessica Davis, and Amy Bowlin (2016) specifically read aloud books involving negative behaviors and social situations; these read alouds help students "learn essential lifelong competencies related to being sensitive to the needs of others, become active problem-solvers, and see themselves as having control over their own life circumstances" (p. 43). Additional therapeutic findings of read alouds follow.

- When students displaying verbal and physical aggression were read to, teachers and students noticed significant behavioral improvements, fewer outbursts, and less negative interactions. The read aloud experience helped students better understand their own feelings and better control their emotional outbursts (Verden, 2012).

- Researchers Eleanor Thompson and Shekila Melchior (2020) find that exposing students to narratives and characters improved their ability to empathize.

As you use read alouds to introduce students to characters, contexts, and situations that either mirror their own realities or offer differing perspectives, you offer opportunities for students to strengthen their humanistic qualities.

The Cognitive and Academic Benefits of Read Alouds

Just as read alouds nurture the physiological and social-emotional sides of students, they also foster students' cognitive and academic growth. A long-standing body of research showcases the manner in which read alouds improve students' language, vocabulary, comprehension, and other academic skills.

There has been tremendous focus in the popular press and on social media about the *science of reading*. This long-standing, interdisciplinary field of research focuses on the cognitive process of how the brain learns to read. Before unpacking how read alouds align with the science of reading, consider exploring an important infographic that pertains to the science of reading. In 2001, Hollis S. Scarborough, senior scientist at Haskins Laboratories, created the *reading rope* to depict reading as a multifaceted intertwining of the many language and literacy skills encompassing word recognition and language comprehension. See an image of the rope at: https://braintrusttutors.com/what-is-the-reading-rope. A well-planned read aloud can strengthen both strands of the rope: students' word-recognition skills and language comprehension. As you read aloud in elementary classrooms, you build students' print awareness by drawing explicit attention to the layout of books and how to maneuver through them: top to bottom, left to right, individual words, punctuation, finger sweeping to a new line, and so on. Print-focused read alouds (I further explore in chapter 3, page 59) help students explore the forms and functions of written language. Read alouds have specific advantages in building the language-comprehension components in the upper strands of Scarborough's (2001) rope. Importantly, read alouds build background knowledge—a foundation on which comprehension stands. As teachers often read aloud from books that may be too difficult for students to independently read, they provide students with rich vocabulary and highlight how syntax and semantics convey the meaning of text. Educators model fluency through intonation, altering their oral delivery to convey meaning and expression, and with appropriate pacing and phrasing. With their myriad of instructional opportunities, read alouds epitomize the translation of the science of reading into classroom practice.

Reading aloud exposes students to novel vocabulary and builds their background knowledge for a variety of topics. A study shows that reading one picture book per day provides young children with exposure to 78,000 words a year (Logan, Justice, Yumuş, & Chapparro-Moreno, 2019). Notably, the words in picture books are often *lexical reservoirs*, meaning they contain a higher number of uncommon words than conversation alone (Mesmer, 2016). Consider the following sentence from Matt de la Peña's (2021) *Milo Imagines the World*: "The whiskered man beside Milo has a face of concentration" (p. 3). Within that one sentence of a read aloud, preschool-aged children would hear *whiskered* and *concentration*—relatively sophisticated words they are unlikely to use in everyday conversation. Thus, as children and young students are read to, their vocabularies expand in both quality and quantity.

Though too often the purview of elementary classrooms exclusively, read alouds are particularly motivating and engaging for older readers. In their survey of nearly two thousand middle schoolers, educators Gay Ivey and Karen Broaddus (2001) report that 62 percent of students chose teacher read alouds over book discussion groups and students reading aloud class novels, plays, or poetry. Overall results indicate the teacher read aloud is one of the most favored activities for reading motivation and school enjoyment. Because middle school classrooms have significant variations of reading levels, read alouds serve as an equalizer, "providing a helpful scaffold for lower ability readers with mature reasoning ability, allowing them to move their concentration from decoding words to the comprehension of new ideas found in texts" (Hurst & Griffity, 2015, p. 46). Jennifer Kohart Marchessault, a faculty member in the School of Education at Grand Canyon State University, and Karen H. Larwin, a professor at Youngstown State University (2014), applied a structured read aloud format to reading interventions and noted positive impacts on middle schoolers' vocabulary and comprehension.

Read alouds are particularly useful in supporting the language development of English learners of varied ages, with positive impacts on motivation, identity, and reading comprehension (Schrodt, Fain, & Hasty, 2015). Read alouds allow students developing language skills to respond to text at multiple levels, thereby improving their vocabulary, comprehension, and language skills (Giroir, Grimaldo, Vaughn, & Roberts, 2015). Do not overlook the conversational and community-based opportunities in read alouds for English learners; as Giroir and colleagues (2015) explain, "When read alouds are enhanced for linguistically diverse students, teachers create a community of learners who use and practice language in meaningful ways, working together to make deeper connections with text" (p. 639). Children's book author and illustrator, Jarrett Lerner, created the engaging illustration in figure I.1. Download the reproducible version to hang in your classroom as a reminder of the benefits of read alouds.

Source: Created by Jarrett Lerner. Used with permission.

Figure I.1: Reading aloud to kids poster.

Visit go.SolutionTree.com/literacy to download this page.

The Motivational Benefits of Read Alouds

The more teachers read aloud to students, the more likely they are to associate reading with joy and pleasure. Readers of all ages report that teacher read alouds are their fondest memories of elementary school (Artley, 1975). Most students show a positive attitude toward reading aloud, with over 75 percent of respondents enjoying being read to (Ledger & Merga, 2018). Students in grades 1–3 (78.9 percent) enjoyed being read to slightly more than students in grades 4–6 (74.4 percent), although the older students still reported enjoying the activity at school. Teachers who alter their voices to emote characters' feelings, deftly display illustrations, encourage conversation and reflection through their text choices, and skillfully select a cliffhanger place to stop (to leave students clambering for tomorrow's read aloud) understand that read alouds are joyful and desirable. As students experience the joy of read alouds, teachers motivate them to engage in their own reading and open them up to the unfamiliar treasures of unread books.

Current Trends in School Read Alouds

Despite the clear social-emotional, cognitive and academic, and motivational benefits for students, the trends show teachers underutilize the read aloud in schools because they do not always fully appreciate its purpose and positive outcomes. A 2022 article by literacy researchers Samuel DeJulio, Miriam Martinez, Janis Harmon, Marcy Wilburn, and Megan Stavinoha analyzed PreK–grade 12 teachers' beliefs about read alouds. More specifically, their survey asked teachers to reflect on the instructional benefits of read alouds (DeJulio et al., 2022). The following patterns about the teachers' beliefs of the purpose of reading aloud emerged among grade levels.

- 25.3 percent of the PreK–grade 2 teachers who took the survey noted their top reason for reading aloud as *interest* and *engagement* (Julio et al., 2022).

- 27 percent of the grades 3–5 teachers who took the survey noted their top reason for reading aloud as *comprehension* (Julio et al., 2022).

- 18 percent of the grades 6–8 teachers who took the survey noted their top reason for reading aloud as *comprehension strategies* (Julio et al., 2022).

So teachers appear aware that read alouds are opportune times to focus on comprehension instruction as well as to pique student interest. In their article, the research team points out "misalignment between research and teachers' beliefs about the purpose of read alouds" (DeJulio et al., 2022, p. 17); they also show only a low percentage of teachers identified content learning, metacognition, and building background knowledge as reasons to read aloud. DeJulio and colleagues (2022) conclude:

> There may be a need for leaders in schools to address read alouds through professional development. Such professional development can help to broaden teachers' perspectives on the ways in which read alouds can foster many different facets of literacy development and can serve as "curriculum bridges" to build background knowledge, establish disciplinary contexts, and promote interest for content learning. (p. 18)

Accordingly, an additional purpose of this book is to remind teachers about the myriad of instructional benefits of read alouds across grade levels.

In 2022, Kristen Smith and her research team set out to explore teachers' rationales for text selection. The subsequent article, "What Are Teachers Reading and Why?" included survey data from 299 first-grade teachers and showed the following trends (Smith, Young, & Yatzeck, 2022).

- Fiction texts dominate teachers' text selections for read alouds (Smith et al., 2022).

- Teachers largely select a text according to their familiarity with it or whether the book is recognized as a classic (Smith et al., 2022).

- Titles read aloud are, on average, twenty-five-years old (Smith et al., 2022).

- Many teachers (50–70 percent) do not often prepare for read alouds (McCaffrey & Hisrich, 2017); teachers seldom plan in advance where to stop during read alouds and what to say when they do stop (Håland, Hoem, & McTigue, 2021).

Because these trends are so important, I look at each of the preceding in greater detail, along with several other important trends.

Text Selections for Read Alouds

When I was in third grade at Pinewood Elementary, my school librarian, Mrs. Ritter, told me there are two types of texts: (1) fiction and (2) nonfiction. In my eight-year-old mind—and for years afterward—I divided books into those that were true (nonfiction) and those that weren't (fiction). Educators have come a long way in considering the forms and genres of texts. Before digging into the trends of read alouds, I'll clarify some overlapping—and often confusing—terminology (see table I.1).

- Generally, texts are divided into types based on their structure and purpose. Those text types are further divided by *genre* according to their form and function (National Literacy Trust, 2013).

- *Narrative* texts are stories, whereas *expository* texts convey information (Hoffman, Teale, & Yokota, 2015; Robinson, 2021). The last text type is *poetry*, with its use of sound, rhythm, imagery, and literary devices (International Literacy Association, n.d.).

- *Informational* text is a subcategory of expository texts; informational text presents information about the natural or social world through *timeless verbs* (Duke, 2000). For example, a timeless verb in an informational text about birds might be the word *chirp* in the phrase *birds chirp*, meaning birds chirped hundreds of years ago just as they chirp today.

Table I.1: Types of Texts

Narrative Text	Expository Text	Poetry
Adventure, mystery, fantasy	Informational text	Free verse
Science fiction	Discussion or explanatory text	Structured
Historical and contemporary fiction	Memoir, biography, autobiography	Visual
Myths, legends, fables, fairy tales		

Consider your classroom library. What kinds of titles might you find on the shelves? Moreover, scan through your last week's read alouds. What kinds of texts did you share? Were your recent read alouds largely narrative, or did you include some informational texts? *Informational text* refers to the specific kind of nonfiction text that uses a non-narrative structure, timeless verbs, and specific vocabulary to tell about the natural or social world. To help teachers and librarians evaluate the quality of their classroom and school libraries, the nonprofit organization First Book created the "Literacy Rich Classroom Library Checklist: An Assessment Tool for Equity" (n.d.). Find it online at https://firstbook.org/solutions/literacy-rich-classrooms, and use it as a way to begin evaluating the diversity of text topic, genre, and format in your classroom library.

In 2000, groundbreaking research from educator Nell K. Duke revealed an extreme shortage of informational texts in classroom libraries and read alouds. Further, early childhood educators and parents reported infrequently reading aloud from informational text (Yopp & Yopp, 2006). Despite publishing houses' concerted push to produce better quality, more engaging informational text, read alouds of informational text still lag behind narrative text (Håland et al., 2021). In a survey of over one thousand grades 1–5 teachers, the teachers self-reported their patterns in selecting text for read alouds (Smith et al., 2022; see table I.2).

Table I.2: Teachers' Self-Reported Inclusion of Read Alouds

Teachers' Selections During Read Alouds	Corresponding Percentage
Inclusion of fiction text	93.7 percent
Featured nonhuman or animal characters	13.2 percent
Use of picture books	35.9 percent
Classified as easy for beginning readers	2.5 percent
Books in verse	0.39 percent
Collections of short stories or poetry	0.73 percent
Bilingual or Spanish books	0.88 percent
Inclusion of nonfiction text	6.0 percent
Use of seasonal text (corresponding to the time of year)	16.2 percent

Source: Adapted from Smith et al., 2022.

Interestingly, researchers Kristin Conradi Smith, Craig A. Young, and Jane Core Yatzeck (2022) point out that although teachers value read alouds, they tend to select dated books. And teachers often make thoughtful text choices that relate to students' interests and identities, but their text choices do not as often address societal concerns, issues of social justice, or reflect a wide lens of diversity. Age-appropriate texts are the most important factor for teachers, with links to specific curriculum units, with theme and length being of lesser importance. That same study reveals 76 percent of teachers report reading aloud from a variety of genres, though they were unlikely to reread the same titles more than once or twice (Smith et al., 2022). Most teachers only reread a book once with each class (19 percent) or twice (34 percent), and approximately 38 percent of teachers read a book three or more times, yet 9 percent of teachers never reread a book (Smith et al., 2022). However, rereading offers great benefits to students, including multiple exposures to vocabulary, deeper comprehension, and opportunities for more sophisticated conversation (O'Connor, Bocian, Beebe-Frankenberger, & Linklater, 2010).

While there are undoubtedly instructional benefits to reading aloud the familiar or classic texts teachers tend to use, O'Connor and colleagues note (2010) teachers cannot overlook the developing explosion of published works which offer reflective and diverse topics, formats, authors, and characters. A 2023 study by Rebecca Giles and Karen Morrison focused on the read aloud choices of prekindergarten teachers. In their survey of 151 teachers, participants reported reading aloud from a self-selected list of 102 books. Of those books, the following patterns emerged: 93 were fiction, and 9 were nonfiction. Most of the texts read aloud were contemporary realistic fiction or folklore. There were very few books read aloud with recent publication dates; only 15 of the texts were published within the last five years. Many holiday books were selected, reflecting Christian and American views. There were almost no multicultural or award-winning books selected. Most participants selected a book because it related to a topic of study; none of the participants reported selecting texts because of their literary quality. When teachers mindfully read aloud from multiple genres, they increase students' ability to synthesize information from a variety of viewpoints and perspectives. Teachers also increase students' background knowledge on topics when they include read alouds from op-eds, how-to manuals, novels in verse, and the many other genres and formats contemporary publications offer. Further, as students grapple with the opportunities and potential obstacles in an increasingly diverse society, it is essential for them to use current texts that reflect current topics. Though there is substantial room for improvement in the diversity of books published yearly— as the annual reports from the Cooperative Children's Book Center at the University of Wisconsin–Madison show (see https://ccbc.education.wisc.edu/literature-resources /ccbc-diversity-statistics)—publications that feature contemporary issues of social justice, identity, and modern trends and issues are impressive. When you only read aloud from familiar or older works, you miss out on the rich conversations, exposure, validation, and learning opportunities more recent texts present. No doubt racism in the classic *To Kill a Mockingbird* (Lee, 1960) uses a different lens than Angie Thomas's 2017 publication *The Hate U Give*.

Plan Time for Read Alouds

As the research demonstrates, most teachers do not often prepare for read alouds, neither spending time on planning the progression of the read aloud or discussion questions nor reading the books ahead of time. In their survey of elementary teachers, McCaffrey and Hisrich (2017) find 50–70 percent of respondents didn't allot intentional planning time for their read alouds. Nearly two-thirds of teacher respondents spent just zero to fifteen minutes *per week* planning read alouds, and two-thirds only sometimes or rarely preview the book in advance (McCaffrey & Hisrich, 2017). Further, an observational study in first-grade classrooms says when teachers do not plan the discussion about the read aloud, they are more likely to ask surface-level questions, clarify content or vocabulary, or ask for simple summarizations—rather than facilitating richer reflections and more complex reactions to text (Håland et al., 2021). This same research team concludes that "the pattern of practices do not reflect a planful and intentional literacy instruction which would systematically support literacy development" (Håland et al., 2021, p. 10).

Discussion Time for Read Alouds

Depending on the type of text, different types of conversations emerge from a read aloud, and this diversity can be valuable. When teachers read from fiction, they typically integrate more turn and talks, read all the words, and provide longer texts (Price, van Kleeck, & Huberty, 2009).

Informational text—with its dense vocabulary, graphic devices that convey information, and abundance of facts—typically leads to conversations with predictions, analysis, and inferring (Moschovaki & Meadows, 2005; Zucker, Justice, Piasta, & Kaderavek, 2010). When early childhood teachers read aloud from informational text, they discuss academic vocabulary and draw explicit attention to text features like maps, headings, and charts (Robinson, 2021). Read alouds of informational texts have fewer student interactions, and when reading these texts, teachers do not adhere to reading every word on the page. While the conversations resulting from read alouds of fiction offer great benefits, those resulting from read alouds of informational text do too. Current trends in read alouds show teachers do not often use informational texts in read alouds, limiting the opportunities for students to have valuable conversations resulting from these texts.

Prevalence of Read Alouds

Even with the wealth of research that supports the social-emotional, cognitive and academic, and motivational benefits of reading aloud to students, an increasing absence of read alouds in classrooms is too often a reality—as in the scene from *Miss Nelson Is Missing!* (Allard, 1977) in the introduction (page 1). The time-honored practice of read alouds is losing its sacred spot in classrooms. According to Scholastic (n.d.), the frequency of reading aloud to elementary school students has significantly dropped since 2014. Scholastic (n.d.) also reports that while 77 percent of teachers set aside time for read alouds, only 36 percent commit to reading aloud every day. A survey reveals that 27 percent of middle school teachers report never reading aloud (Ariail & Albright, 2006). Data from Scholastic (n.d.) note while 61 percent of elementary teachers read aloud daily, only 23 percent of middle school and 7 percent of high school teachers do the same. In fact, 47 percent of high school teachers report *never* reading aloud. The pressure of high-stakes tests limits many well-intentioned teachers, who are bound to scripted curricula and test prep materials (Merga & Ledger, 2019).

The Need for Read Alouds in Everyday Classroom Instruction

All students (and younger children) need the experience of having an adult read to them to access the benefits of read alouds. Outside school, read alouds may not be routine occurrences for all students. Many well-intentioned parents face overwhelming challenges (as such, a bedtime story might fall to the lower rungs of their priority list). Other parents and caregivers might have their own negative associations with schooling or literacy, and are unenthusiastic about reading at home. Other families lack access to books and libraries (Ness, 2019a). In a 2019 study, researchers counted books available for purchase in various neighborhoods to determine students' access to age-appropriate resources (Neuman & Moland, 2019). Stark disparities emerged between the students' access to books based on the socioeconomic status of their neighborhoods, with 830 students having to share one book in low-income neighborhoods versus only two students sharing a book in high-income areas (Neuman & Moland, 2019).

The following data depict that not every student reaps the benefits of frequent read alouds at home.

- In a sample of 8,900 children, one-fourth of four-year-olds were never read to at home (Khan, Purtell, Logan, Ansari, & Justice, 2017).

- During the school closures associated with COVID-19, 27 percent of teachers report they encouraged families to read aloud, while only 5 percent of teachers believe read aloud time happened more often during the COVID-19 school disruption. Half of teachers reported not knowing the extent of home read alouds at all (Scholastic, n.d.).

When students lack reading experiences at home, they experience a *word gap*—the massive differences in heard vocabulary between disadvantaged and advantaged children in their first five years of life (Logan et al., 2019). This same research team posits that incoming kindergarten students from literacy-rich homes hear a cumulative 1.4 million more words than students who never have storybook reading time (Logan et al., 2019). The following information demonstrates how students who are frequently read to at home hear far more words than students with infrequent home read alouds.

- Children who are read to daily in the birth to one-year-old range hear about 46,956 words per year while those read to less often hear fewer: 3–5 times per week, 26,832; 1–2 times per week, 10,062; less than once a week, 738 (Logan et al., 2019).

- Children who are read to daily in the one- to two-year-old range hear about 93,912 words per year while those read to less often hear fewer: 3–5 times per week, 53,664; 1–2 times per week, 20,124; less than once a week, 1,476 (Logan et al., 2019).

- Children who are read to daily in the two- to three-year-old range hear about 140,868 words per year while those read to less often hear fewer: 3–5 times per week, 80,496; 1–2 times per week, 30,186; less than once a week, 2,214 (Logan et al., 2019).

- Children who are read to daily in the three- to four-year-old range hear about 218,764 words per year while those read to less often hear fewer: 3–5 times per week, 125,008; 1–2 times per week, 46,878; less than once a week, 3,435 (Logan et al., 2019).

- Children who are read to daily in the four- to five-year-old range hear about 296,660 words per year while those read to less often hear fewer: 3–5 times per week, 169,520; 1–2 times per week, 63,570; less than once a week, 4,662 (Logan et al., 2019).

If educators disaggregated every moment in students' lives, they would discover that school-aged children spend nearly 87 percent of their time outside school (though this statistic does not differentiate between waking and sleeping minutes) (Wherry, 2004). Since students' home environments are beyond schools' locus of control, *educators must ensure read alouds are a non-negotiable part of daily classroom instruction*—for all students in all grades and all content areas. According to Scholastic (n.d.), this is not yet the case: while 77 percent of teachers set time aside for independent reading or read aloud time, only 36 percent do this every school day.

Though my hope is educators everywhere will carve out time and space for a read aloud in every PreK–8 classroom every day, I am in no way suggesting read alouds take the place of explicit reading instruction. In addition to listening to a read aloud—be it in a kindergarten classroom with a rich storybook or a seventh-grade social studies classroom with an important historical figure's speech—students need significant teacher-led instruction on both reading skills (for example, word recognition, vocabulary, making meaning, fluency, and writing) and domain-specific knowledge. Research indicates about 58 percent of the school day is allocated to academic activities; of that allotted instructional time, only one-third is spent working with an adult, with the remaining two-thirds consisting of seatwork (Rosenshine, 2015). While read alouds are essential, they must not take the place of the essential time teachers need to teach reading. Reading expert Timothy Shanahan (2022) writes:

> Reading to children is not a particularly effective way of teaching reading. However, there are several ways that shared reading can be used as a mechanism to accomplish some specific goals in the primary grades. It can both be an extracurricular activity aimed at warming up a classroom or it may be a tool aimed at teaching or familiarizing students with some very specific aspects of reading ability. What it should not be is the way students learn to read a particular text, nor should it replace instruction in which students would usually be expected to do the reading.

In my ideal rich reading environment in a PreK–8 classroom, both thoughtful reading instruction and rich immersive read alouds occur daily. My book addresses one-half of that ideal by offering the planning steps to develop effective read alouds.

About This Book

Whether you come to this book committed to and experienced in supporting the benefits of read alouds in PreK–8 classrooms or are relatively new to read alouds—perhaps hoping to introduce them in your daily routine with your students but unsure of how to fit them in—this book offers the tools to begin or enrich reading aloud to your students. These tools, along with comprehensive instructions for application and research-supported information on the importance and varied benefits of the read aloud, are available over four sequential chapters. Chapter 1, "Plan the Read Aloud," articulates a three-step process for planning the read aloud. This process includes information on how to (1) evaluate texts, (2) explain texts to students to aid comprehension (through such practices as modeling critical thinking by wondering aloud and teaching vocabulary), and (3) engage and extend the impact of a text by focusing on social-emotional learning, cross-curricular connections, and supporting further reading and writing. Chapter 2, "Apply the Read Aloud Plan to Diverse Texts," offers examples of the three-step process applied to three different texts, each for a different grade segment (PreK–2, 3–5, and 6–8). Chapter 3, "Use Age-Appropriate Read Aloud Strategies" encompasses strategies for increasing the read aloud's impact by tailoring it to specific grade levels and developmental stages and exploring practices such as using visualization to aid the comprehension of preschool and early elementary students to encouraging student-generated questions. Chapter 4, "Customize Read Alouds for Various Content Areas," opens with a discussion of the need for read alouds in science, mathematics, and other classes beyond the language arts. It notes the difference in how often teachers offer read alouds in language arts classes versus other classes and provides a condensed version of the planning process chapter 1 outlines. I focus on bringing read alouds to science, mathematics, physical education, art, and other special classes.

In addition to the sequential content of the chapters, the section A Call to Action appears at the end of each chapter, offering chapter content-related questions to encourage readers to reflect on past experiences of reading aloud to students and consider how they might apply new strategies from the book to future read alouds. The book closes with an epilogue and appendices that offer additional forms of support, including lists of potential texts for read alouds, online sources for information about choosing content-focused material, and more. At many points throughout the book, I invite readers into my thinking process in planning a read aloud. I model this process as both approachable and variable rather than a process with fixed rules or that needs to adhere to some notion of "perfect."

While planning a read aloud might feel overwhelming, the strategies, information, and planning guidelines in this book aim to streamline the process and make it feel possible and rewarding. I hope to show that, in essence, a well-conducted read aloud is elegant in its simplicity—all teachers need to start is a student, an adult reader, and a beloved text. Despite simple inputs, the outputs are extraordinary at an interdisciplinary, holistic level—cognitively, social-emotionally, developmentally, and linguistically. My hope is this book will activate your joy in reading aloud, so you embrace reading aloud to your students not as something you *have* to do but rather as something you *get* to do. As coauthors Saba K. Vlach, Tova S. Lentz, and Gholnecsar E. Muhammad explain in their 2023 article, "Teachers can begin their journey toward joy by activating joy for their students and themselves during their daily read-aloud practice" (p. 9). I hope this book reminds you of the power of read alouds, as well as introduces groundbreaking science that will ignite or reignite your commitment to reading aloud. Once educators understand the richness of read alouds, they can embrace them as an essential component in the development of every student.

Plan the Read Aloud

When I was a first-year middle school teacher in Oakland, California, I started my new position with a passion for reading and an eagerness to share the joys of reading with my soon-to-be students. When I arrived, however, I found my school's library permanently shuttered. I was given $400 to fund my own classroom library, which I did in the only space available, a ramshackle bookshelf in the corner of my classroom.

My sixth-grade students spoke nearly a dozen languages, and I was lost, ill prepared, lacking resources, and facing significant language barriers. One thing I instinctually knew, however, was that I had to read aloud daily to my students. Our read aloud occurred at the same time every day—when my students returned, sweaty and rambunctious, from the antics, excitement, and drama that had unfolded in a back-to-back lunch and recess block. At the time, I didn't know about the research supporting read alouds; I simply realized the read aloud provided a time for my students to unwind, cool down, and transition from the revved-up lunch and recess block to a focused learning time.

Admittedly, I made some mistakes during my early read alouds. First, I chose each book, and my choices relied solely on the selections being some of my beloved childhood favorites. I did not consult my students on what they might like to hear, nor did I comb through the myriad of book lists, awards, or websites featuring engaging, diverse texts (which you can find in appendices C, D, and E, pages 107, 109, and 113). Yet, I quickly learned that just because I had enjoyed Gary Paulsen's (1999) *Hatchet* did not mean my students would too. Much to my chagrin, *Hatchet* was a total flop—its slow, unfolding action bored my students, who had no interest in nature survival stories (perhaps because they had no significant exposure to nature, and survivor-themed plots were not yet popular in television or movies). So while I gave up *Hatchet* midway through the read aloud, my students begged me to read for more than the allotted fifteen minutes when our text was S. E. Hinton's (1967) *The Outsiders*.

Another big no-no? I failed to preview each text in its entirety before I read it aloud. When a particularly poignant moment unfolded in Andrew Clements's (1996) *Frindle*, my students were gobsmacked to find me reacting with sentimental tears. My biggest mistake was my overarching lack of planning in my read aloud. My planning was limited to previewing the pages I anticipated my class and I would cover over a week of instruction and selecting some vocabulary words to teach. In fact, as a rookie teacher, I believed planning my read aloud entailed determining how many pages I'd read and an appropriate stopping point.

Years later, I'm able to look past my well-intentioned mistakes and focus on the powerful instructional and social-emotional opportunities that reading aloud provided my students. For many of my students, the read aloud was the most joyful part of the school day. Many students read well below grade level and struggled in their content-area classrooms to understand textbooks. They did not identify as readers, and reported they hated to read; yet these same students were rapt as Charlie and his grandfather met Willy Wonka, as the wonders of Narnia unfolded, and as sisters Beezus and Ramona squabbled. For many, listening to books is more pleasant and relaxing than actually reading books (Best, Clark, & Picton, 2020; McGeown, Bonsall, Andries, Howarth, & Wilkinson, 2020).

Later, I discovered my lack of planning read alouds is quite common. Though many have written on the need to effectively plan read alouds (Fisher, Flood, Lapp, & Frey, 2004; Ness, 2018), many teachers (50–70 percent) do not often prepare for read alouds, meaning they either do not plan the instructional sequence of the read aloud or read the book ahead of time (McCaffrey & Hisrich, 2017). This chapter addresses that lack of planning and aims to provide effective ideas and strategies to efficiently plan read alouds. The chapter does this by guiding readers through the three-step process I developed to plan my own PreK–8 read alouds. Each of these three steps—(1) evaluate, (2) explain, and (3) engage and extend—includes several smaller steps, each of which I'll visit in its own subsection. Prior to moving through each step and mini-step, I introduce the reproducible "Read Aloud Planning Template" (see the reproducible version in appendix A, page 102) to use as a guide for the content in this book and your future read aloud planning. I next walk through completing the corresponding section of the read aloud planning template, using the picture book, *Knuffle Bunny: A Cautionary Tale* (Willems, 2004) as an example. Finally, at the end of the chapter, you will find the repeating A Call to Action section with questions for reflection on chapter content.

The Three-Step Process for Planning Your Read Aloud

Once I made the realization—drawn both from research and my own teaching experience—that read alouds are largely unplanned instructional activities, I devised a process to intentionally plan my read alouds. In the nearly two decades I have spent as a university professor and teacher educator, I have introduced this process to the hundreds of preservice and early career teachers who enrolled in my literacy methods classes. While the planning process steps contain multiple mini-steps, here's an overview of the process. Please note: I intentionally do not include the complicated process of text selection in my process (see appendix D, page 109, for a list wonderful titles). I pick up at the point

Do Audiobooks Count as Read Alouds?

I'd like to weigh in on an ongoing debate. I am frequently asked if listening to a book—as in *audiobooks* (my 'tween daughter gets very irritated when I refer to them as "books on tape")—counts as reading. This debate came up when my daughter's elementary school began its annual read-a-thon fundraiser. Do the minutes students listened to a book count on their reading logs? My hunch is this debate emerges from the belief that listening is more passive than reading, and with that argument, listening to books counts as cheating or as not real reading (Clark, 2007; Moyer, 2011).

Undoubtedly, audiobooks have undergone an uptick in popularity, ease, and access; apps like Libby (https://help.libbyapp.com/en-us/6103.htm), Audible (https://audible.com), LibroFM (https://libro.fm/guide), and Hoopla (https://hoopla.com) make your favorite John Grisham or Ernest Hemingway tomes portable and instantly accessible. The Audio Publishers Association reports that the audiobook market has increased by double digits in sales in the past few years (Maughan, 2022). More than 50 percent of patrons ages twelve and older have listened to an audiobook in the past twelve months (National Public Media, 2022). Additionally, audiobooks offer a model of strong prosody, intonation, and inflection, enabling listeners to better comprehend text. With the ability to control the speed of delivery, listeners can also access a text at a pace that suits their preference. Further, audiobooks afford learners the chance to access text when reading a hard copy is not an option; my favorite times to "read" with audiobooks are as I fold laundry, shower, and walk the dog (all possible with my smartphone and earbuds!). It's no wonder school systems spend some of their precious funding to support students with access to diverse, engaging audiobook libraries.

Science indicates there are no reliable differences between reading and listening comprehension (Clinton, 2019). In other words, the brain does not process the words you hear or the words you read differently, therefore myth-busting the notion that listening to books is cheating. In fact, audiobooks offer unique advantages: they allow readers to access texts that may exceed their decoding abilities and serve as a powerful model of fluency, as audiobooks are recorded with deliberate attention to intonation, prosody, and expression.

However, educators should be mindful: listening to an audiobook may not offer the personalized connection present in a teacher-led read aloud. After all, when a teacher reads aloud to the class, that teacher has the power to pause and make a thoughtful connection between the text and something of relevance to that particular group of students, for instance. The teacher modifies the read aloud on visual cues from students, pausing when students appear puzzled, hamming it up at comical points, or even skipping over lengthy passages when students appear bored. In other words, audiobooks offer particular instructional opportunities but may not deliver the warmth of shared moments between a teacher and students. Nonetheless, as reading "rock star" and cognitive psychologist Daniel Willingham says, "I say don't feel a little bit ashamed. . . . Fly your audiobook flag proudly" (as cited in Dohms, 2019).

at which I've already selected the text to read. I will say, however, foremost in my mind in the process of text selection is the relevance of text—relevance to both my students (interests and identities) and relevance to my content and teaching objectives.

- **Step one: Evaluate.** Evaluate the text for the background knowledge it assumes the reader brings. Be mindful of the *funds of knowledge*—or the cultural capital (see page 23)—necessary for readers to understand the text. Become aware of the opportunities and obstacles in each text—opportunities for literacy and extracurricular extensions, as well as potential obstacles that might impede students' understanding of the text.

- **Step two: Explain.** Incorporate *think alouds*—the purposeful use of *I language* to model how you are making meaning from the text (Ness, 2018). Be mindful of novel vocabulary words—both the words you choose to provide meaningful instruction on and the words you can simply explain (so as to not hinder comprehension of overall content).

- **Step three: Engage and Extend.** Whereas step two, explain, is largely teacher driven, this final step shifts responsibility back to students. Here, teachers engage students in critical inquiry and reflection about the text. They extend opportunities to further students' critical thinking through literacy-rich extensions and engage students in rich conversations.

These three steps empower teachers to pinpoint potential points of confusion, intentionally amplify the text's instructional opportunities, and offer scaffolds to improve students' understanding—and ultimate enjoyment—of a text.

As you think through the evaluate, explain, and engage and extend phases of planning, use this read aloud planning template to make your thinking tangible (see figure 1.1) The headings you see in the template support the mini-steps in my three-step process. Under these headings, add the resulting content of your thought process for planning.

In the following sections, I'll discuss the components of the three-step process for planning a read aloud using *Knuffle Bunny: A Cautionary Tale* (Willems, 2004) throughout to serve as an example for how to think about a text for a read aloud. After discussing the three components separately, I'll generate content to complete the template by drawing from *Knuffle Bunny*.

Evaluate

When you first peruse a text, your intent should be to identify anything that might potentially trip up students or deter their comprehension. The barriers to comprehension are often (1) unfamiliar vocabulary and (2) background knowledge the text assumes a reader brings to the page. Your role in the evaluate step is to act as a detective, sorting out what might be problematic so you can set up your students for success. If you know where the potential pitfalls are, you can help your students avoid them—either through explicit modeling, preteaching, or additional scaffolding. This preparatory process is one teachers do for many activities in their everyday lives, yet they often leapfrog over it in reading. If you see ominous clouds in the sky, you toss an umbrella in your bag. If you're about to embark upon a long drive, you'll load up your phone with audiobooks and pack extra snacks. Similarly, if you know there is unfamiliar vocabulary in your read aloud, you'll anticipate which words to preteach. In a fourth-grade read aloud of a historical fiction picture book, anticipate how to front-load information about the relevant time period to set up students for success.

Title of Text:			

Evaluate

Background Knowledge

Funds of Knowledge

Potential Stumbling Blocks

Instructional Opportunities

Explain

Brainstorm Unfamiliar Words

Words to Teach	Short, Simple, Straightforward Definitions	Words to Explain	Short, Simple, Straightforward Definitions

Think Alouds

Stopping or Pausing Points	I Language

Engage and Extend

Social-Emotional Learning Engagement

Cross-Curricular Extensions

Extensions to Support Reading and Writing

Figure 1.1: Read aloud planning template.

Visit go.SolutionTree.com/literacy to download this page.

Next, examine how to evaluate texts for read alouds by considering that process in its component parts. Each component corresponds to the following sections of the read aloud planning template: (1) background knowledge, (2) funds of knowledge, (3) potential stumbling blocks, and (4) instructional opportunities.

Assess Necessary Background Knowledge

First, look critically at what information, experiences, or knowledge student readers must have to successfully understand the book. Ask yourself the following questions, for example.

- "What do students need to know about the topic before reading this book?"

- "Are there locations, references, interactions, events, or experiences in the book students are likely unfamiliar with?"

Central to reading aloud is fostering students' comprehension, or meaning making, of each text. Reading comprehension is a complex, multifaceted construct that is both highly individualistic and dependent on the reader, the text, and the purpose for reading (Snow, 2000). In a 2022 article, professor, researcher, and author, Hugh W. Catts reminds teachers:

> Reading comprehension is not a skill someone learns and can then apply in different reading contexts. It is one of the most complex activities that we engage in on a regular basis, and our ability to comprehend is dependent upon a wide range of knowledge and skills. (p. 27)

A wide body of research suggests *background knowledge* supports students' comprehension during and after reading (Cervetti & Wright, 2020). Background knowledge supports comprehension in several ways. As education journalist Natalie Wexler (2019) explains, background knowledge serves as a magnet to make new learning stick; when people know a bit about a topic, they are more likely to anchor new information to previously known knowledge. This enables readers to draw inferences about missing information and ideas not explicitly explained. Or, as discussed in *schemata theory*, people are more likely to retain and transfer information if they already have some foundational knowledge of the concept (Anderson, 1984). Additionally, background knowledge facilitates thinking about text by placing less of a burden on working (or short-term) memory.

Understandably, much focus has been placed on the ways teachers activate and build students' background knowledge (Cabell & Hwang, 2020; Cervetti & Wright, 2020; Wexler, 2019), and building this background knowledge is foundational work in the evaluate phase of my read aloud planning template. Background knowledge, however, is just a small part of the knowledge and skills students bring to the classroom. If only there were a clear-cut way to accurately measure students' background knowledge on the wide variety of topics they are likely to encounter! Instead, teachers must rely on their own knowledge of their students' home lives, interests, cultures, and educational backgrounds. For instance, a fourth-grade teacher about to begin a unit on marine life might consider what field trips students engaged in in previous grades, what movies or television shows might relate, and where students spend their out-of-classroom time. The background knowledge students bring to the classroom is highly personal, and learning about students' interests and experiences is an important part of evaluating what they know.

Consider Funds of Knowledge

While background knowledge focuses on content and topics related to ideas a text presents, students also bring to school certain understandings of social norms, ways of interaction, and cultural elements they have learned and use to navigate in their everyday lives. These norms, ways, and cultural elements can differ greatly from one student to the next and are called *funds of knowledge*, an entity that may overlap with, but may also differ from, background knowledge. Funds of knowledge convey the notion that families—particularly those from working-class and low-income backgrounds—have produced and acquired knowledge, social norms, practices, and experiences in their homes and communities.

I'll explore the notion of funds of knowledge with a few examples. Consider the ways of meeting people for the first time, and the relevant funds of knowledge. In the United States, people typically shake hands with someone they've just met. But in some Asian cultures, people bow as sign of greeting, whereas many Europeans lightly kiss an acquaintance on both cheeks. All these cultural interactions call on funds of knowledge; they draw on social norms. Funds of knowledge also exist within families; chances are my Thanksgiving table looks different from my neighbors', as people each incorporate special dishes, mementos, and traditions unique to their families and communities. Knowing how to navigate those contexts—both greeting people and sharing a holiday meal—helps people alter their own behavior so it fits in and improves their acceptance. The same is true for the funds of knowledge a text brings, only here teachers improve their chance of building students' comprehension.

Researchers Luis C. Moll, Cathy Amanti, Deborah Neff, and Norma Gonzalez (1992) coined the term *funds of knowledge*; they refer to funds of knowledge as "the historically accumulated and culturally developed bodies of knowledge and skills essential for household or individual functioning and well-being" (p. 133). To begin considering the funds of knowledge a text assumes its readers possess, ask yourself the following questions.

- "What does the book assume readers bring to the page with them?"
- "What settings and interactions are included in the book, and what are the associated funds of knowledge?"
- "Are there elements of a character's background, culture, or community that might be unfamiliar to readers?"

While background knowledge and funds of knowledge certainly overlap, they are not the same thing; whereas *background knowledge* is what students know from their academic and personal experiences, *funds of knowledge* intentionally honor the experiences and assets students bring from their cultures, families, and communities. The word *fund* stems from the French word *fond*, meaning a bottom, floor, or ground. Thus, funds of knowledge remind teachers that students carry knowledge they've gained simply through living their lives; that knowledge is a foundation on which schools must build.

To give an example of how to consider funds of knowledge when evaluating a text to prepare for a read aloud, I'll jump ahead here to author, illustrator, animator, and playwright Mo Willems's (2004) *Knuffle Bunny: A Cautionary Tale*. I'll look at how the funds of knowledge this text assumes may align (or not) with those of your students and how to address a potential alignment gap.

Knuffle Bunny tells the story of Trixie, a precocious toddler, her patient father, and their adventure down the block, past the school, to the laundromat. Trixie carries her beloved stuffed rabbit, Knuffle Bunny, which she clutches tightly in her hand on her trip to the laundromat. Once at the laundromat, Trixie plays as her father loads the laundry and puts money into the washing machine. But on the return home, she is verklempt to discover Knuffle Bunny is missing. Thwarted by *toddler-ese*, Trixie's father cannot understand why Trixie is so upset. Though her father pleads with her not to get fussy, Trixie melts down in tears and has a tantrum. The father-daughter duo arrives home unhappy, and immediately, Trixie's mother recognizes Knuffle Bunny's disappearance. The three run back to the laundromat, and after several tries, the father finds the toy among the wet laundry and claims hero status. The girl exclaims, "Knuffle Bunny!!!"—her first clear spoken words (Willems, 2004, p. 32).

Undoubtedly, *Knuffle Bunny* contains background knowledge the reader needs to fully comprehend the text. The book takes place in the heart of Brooklyn, and readers will better understand the story if they are familiar with the layout of an urban neighborhood. Most importantly, readers need to understand a laundromat as a public space where anyone can do laundry; this setting may be unfamiliar to students who have a washer and dryer in their own homes or apartment buildings.

But the book also relies on a reader's funds of knowledge, or social capital. Here are the funds of knowledge specific to *Knuffle Bunny* (Willems, 2004).

- The sharing of domestic chores (Trixie's father doing the laundry while her mother stays home)

- A beloved stuffed animal holding an important role in childhood

- The give and take of language as Trixie's father tries to understand Trixie's preschool language

All these elements of background knowledge and funds of knowledge serve as potential stumbling blocks for readers. If students have never set foot in a laundromat, they might fail to understand the ways in which Trixie amuses herself as her father works. If a treasured stuffed animal is not a part of their childhood culture, students might not grasp why Trixie's family searches desperately for the lost Knuffle Bunny. But once the teacher pinpoints these potential stumbling blocks, they can take the necessary precautions to prepare students to access the content. Teachers might preteach what a laundromat is—through photos or quick videos. They might ask students to share out the names of their favorite stuffed animals and imagine how they'd react if they were lost. While I'm focusing here on just two specific examples from the larger text, the underlying notion is teachers must consider what ideas, experiences, and knowledge will help students to better understand the text. The big idea here is as teachers evaluate the text prior to reading, they can pinpoint the background knowledge and funds of knowledge that might be problematic if they do not deliberately address them. When teachers focus solely on background knowledge, they overlook the richness of students' life experiences and their foundational role in learning.

Address Potential Stumbling Blocks

As I discussed previously, when teachers consider who students are as individuals and the knowledge they bring to the classroom, they become more aware of potential gaps between students' understandings and the text. By becoming aware of these gaps, teachers are more likely to recognize them as points of confusion for students. However, there are additional reasons texts might confuse students. These include language, settings, sequence of events, inferences, and so on. I recall reading aloud author Louis Sachar's (2000) beloved book *Holes* to a group of fourth graders. The book essentially has two timelines that overlap by a common setting: one storyline follows the contemporary protagonist Stanley Yelnats as he goes to Camp Green Lake, while another storyline follows a schoolteacher-turned-bandit in the 1920s. As I read, I became painfully aware that students struggled to follow the unannounced switch in timeline and the lack of clarity on how the timelines come together. Had I evaluated the text more comprehensively in my planning, I might simply have mapped out a chart of the two timelines to alert readers as to what action was unfolding when.

When examining the challenges a text might present to students, it is essential to make that examination comprehensive and consider how to proactively address stumbling blocks such as multiple timelines, flashbacks, changing points of view, and so much more. Ask yourself the following questions.

- "Where else in the text might readers struggle? What potential points of confusion are there?" Be careful about multiple characters, changes in settings (locations and time frames), and additional tricky spots.
- "What experiences, knowledge, explanation, or exposure can I build, enhance, or lend my students in advance of reading?"
- "What ways (for example, conversation, demonstration, or photographs or video explanations) can I enhance students' background knowledge and funds of knowledge?"

Consider Texts for Instructional Opportunities

Just as teachers should draw awareness to the challenges a text presents, they should aim to be equally mindful of its opportunities. Select a text for a read aloud for a certain purpose—either because it aligns with overarching instruction, is a mentor text for a particular literacy strategy, or perhaps resonates with your students' social-emotional needs. Now is your chance to shine the light on the text itself and enhance its offerings.

As you preview the text, make mindful notes about where you want to draw students' attention, ways to draw out conversations after reading, and themes, concepts, and language you aim to revisit. Ask yourself questions such as the following to help uncover the text's instructional opportunities.

- "What lessons, conversations, and follow-up activities jump to mind?"
- "How might I take advantage of these opportunities?"

Remember my early reference to *Miss Nelson Is Missing!* (Allard, 1977), the ubiquitous picture book in which a sweet, mild-natured teacher disguises herself as a strict substitute teacher? This book, for example, offers the perfect opportunity to help students make inferences. They combine text clues with their background knowledge to make educated assumptions about the text. As you evaluate the text, simply jot down *modeling of inferences and their importance in reading* as an instructional opportunity. This serves as a reminder of where you might focus your follow-up planning.

After selecting your read aloud, examine the text for the background knowledge and funds of knowledge the text assumes the reader brings to the page, considering additional comprehension stumbling blocks and opportunities embedded in the text. Now you're ready to fill out the top portion, Evaluate, of the read aloud planning template (see figure 1.2). Simply jot quick notes to yourself, as this is not meant to be a time-consuming word-for-word transcript of your instructional plan.

Now that you have a clear sense of what the text you chose offers (both its challenges and opportunities), you are ready to think through and plan how to respond to and best utilize these challenges and opportunities for students in the second step (explain).

Title of Text: Jot down your title here. The intent is to create a planning guide you can swap with your colleagues to share an entire library of read alouds.

Example: Knuffle Bunny

Evaluate

Background Knowledge

Jot down quick bullet points of what you see as the background knowledge the text requires. If it's also useful, make quick notes of how you might build or activate that knowledge.

Example:

- The setting is a city neighborhood, where people often walk or take buses instead of driving cars.
- A laundromat is a public space where anyone can do laundry; in cities people often use laundromats because they are more likely to not have a washer or dryer in their smaller apartments.

Show picture of laundromat on a SMART Board (or similar tool) since it will be a new location for some students.

Have students draw maps of their own neighborhoods and discuss differences.

Funds of Knowledge

Jot down quick bullet points of what you see as the funds of knowledge the text assumes. You might notice an overlap with the background knowledge.

Example:

- Trixie's mom and dad share the chores in the house. Trixie's father does the laundry while her mother stays home.
- Some children cherish a beloved stuffed animal; for Trixie, it is her stuffed animal called Knuffle Bunny.
- Sometimes adults have a hard time understanding young children as they talk.

Potential Stumbling Blocks

Here, make quick notes of any parts, ideas, or text elements that might confuse students. Simply list them here to jump-start your thinking about how to handle them.

Example:

- Students might be confused as they try to understand Trixie's preschool language.
- Students might not understand why Trixie is so unhappy.
- Students might be confused by the figurative use of the expression went boneless.

Instructional Opportunities

To remind yourself of the intended reasons you selected this text, quickly jot down conversation starters, reflective questions, social-emotional links, curricular extensions, and other opportunities so you are mindful of the richness of the text.

Example:

- This is a chance to tap into students' social-emotional learning—make connections to times they've felt angry.
- There are opportunities in the text to model inferencing, such as looking at pictures of Trixie's facial expressions and asking, "How do you think she feels?" or "How might Trixie's mommy and daddy be feeling as they search for Knuffle Bunny?"

Source: Willems, 2004.

Figure 1.2: How to use the read aloud planning template for the evaluate step.

Explain

In the second step, provide rich explanations to students in two specific areas: (1) the lingering comprehension roadblocks you identified in the first step, and (2) the unfamiliar vocabulary that helps unlock meaning for students. Once you evaluate the text to consider where readers might struggle, reframe your read aloud as an opportunity to build comprehension. I'll begin with the ever-important vocabulary.

Explain Unfamiliar Vocabulary

The link between vocabulary and comprehension is undeniable; if readers can't identify the words in a text, they cannot understand the text. A rich body of research highlights that vocabulary knowledge relates to—and even predicts—reading comprehension (Beck, McKeown, & Kucan, 2013; Cunningham & Stanovich, 1997). Researchers and professors of education Anne E. Cunningham and Keith E. Stanovich (1997) designed an amazing milestone longitudinal study. For this study, a group of first graders underwent a battery of reading assessments—including assessments on foundational skills, vocabulary knowledge, cognitive skills, and comprehension. These same students took tests in reading comprehension, general knowledge, and vocabulary—*ten years later*. The results show a strong correlation between students' first-grade vocabulary knowledge and their high school reading comprehension! World of Words (n.d.) notes, "Effective vocabulary intervention can essentially erase reading difficulties later on. . . . The quantity, quality, and responsiveness of teacher talk can significantly improve children's receptive and expressive vocabulary."

Read alouds are also an optimal point for vocabulary instruction because of their *lexical richness* (that is, their wealth of uncommon words). A 2019 study evaluated the inclusion of rare words in children's literature and found that of every 1,000 words, 30.9 are rare (Logan et al., 2019). Consider this: children's books contain more rare words than prime-time television shows for adults (22.7 of 1,000) and children (20.2 of 1,000) alike, and even more than college graduates' conversational speech (17.3 of 1,000; Logan et al., 2019).

These data suggest reading aloud "creates an environment in which children are exposed to more unique words than they would be through speech alone" (Montag, Jones, & Smith, 2015, p. 1494). Without the rich instructional opportunities read alouds offer, students' vocabulary exposure might merely come from decontextualized workbook instruction or isolated word lists to memorize (Hiebert, 2019). In fact, read alouds—with direct vocabulary support—promote vocabulary growth (Wasik, Hindman, & Snell, 2016).

Recall the example from de la Peña's (2021) *Milo Imagines the World* in the introduction (page 7), or consider a second example of opportunities to explore rich vocabulary in children's books with this one simple sentence from William Steig's (1998) *Pete's a Pizza*: "Pete's father can't help noticing how miserable his son is" (p. 4). This relatively simple book tells of young Pete, who is disappointed that the rain has thwarted his outdoor play. In one sentence, there are two rich vocabulary words that are both novel and introduce lexical richness: *noticing* and *miserable*. Though these words may be unfamiliar to students, they still are understandable. *Noticing* is a more sophisticated and nuanced way to say seeing or observing; you can easily define *miserable* as unhappy. Because children as

Words to Teach Versus Words to Explain

Not sure of when to teach a word and when to explain it? To help differentiate between the two, ask yourself, "Is this a word my students are likely to use in their everyday lives? Will they add it to their expressive vocabulary? Am I likely to see it in their journals or to overhear it at lunchtime conversations?" If you answer *yes* to these questions, it's a word to teach. If not, that word is more likely a word to explain.

Here's an example from author William Steig's (1986) *Brave Irene*. This picture book tells of a young girl named Irene, who helps her sick mother by delivering a package during a winter storm. In the package is a dress her mother—a seamstress—made for an upcoming ball. Complimenting the handiwork, Irene tells her mother, "The duchess will love it!" The word *duchess* is a prime example of a word to explain rather than teach; in almost no time, you can tell your students *duchess* is another word for *princess*—as they will likely have already heard of a princess (Thank you, Disney!). Because a duchess is largely irrelevant to their everyday lives, don't commit extended instructional time to this word. Be mindful of your students' everyday lives. However, if you happen to teach in an area where there actually is a duchess, this word might be a word to teach!

If duchess is not a word to teach, you might select another word that appears later in this same text: *errand*. Because this word is relevant and useful in everyday conversation, you might provide deeper instruction here to showcase that an errand is a kind of job that someone asks someone else to do. You might ask your classroom helper to *run an errand* for you by delivering something to the office, or encourage students to think about the errands they run on the weekend with their families or caregivers.

young as preschoolers already have the foundational understandings of these words, they are able to use them in their everyday expressive vocabularies. Coauthors Isabel L. Beck, Margaret G. McKeown, and Linda Kucan (2013) would label *miserable* and *noticing* as Tier 2 words—or more sophisticated ways to label ideas or concepts students already know. While it may be unreasonable for young students such as those in PreK through the earliest elementary grades to write these words independently, they can use them in conversation and understand them through reading and particularly through the vocabulary instruction opportunities that stem from read alouds.

Accordingly, in this second phase of read aloud planning, teachers should evaluate for unfamiliar vocabulary and then adhere to the following principles of effective vocabulary instruction.

- Choose target vocabulary words ahead of the read aloud (Hadley & Mendez, 2021). Researchers Tanya S. Wright and Susan B. Neuman (2014) remind educators that teaching words on the fly too often leads to poor word choice, insufficient definitions of words, and insufficient examples of the words in other contexts.

- Focus on *just-right* words. *Just-right words* are words you find in the vocabulary of proficient readers; these words are often more sophisticated ways to identify simple concepts. For example, almost every kindergartner knows the word *happy*. Some just-right words for this simple concept might be *enthusiastic, satisfied,* or *elated*. To avoid feeling totally overwhelmed in vocabulary instruction, evaluate for two types of words: (1) words to teach and (2) words to explain. The following lists are meant to aid in delineating these two types of words in a text.

Words to teach:

- Neither too easy nor too difficult

- Useful to students

- Likely for students to use in their everyday speaking and writing

- Brings students closer to developing sophisticated lexicons (Beck et al., 2013; Biemiller, 2010; Hadley & Mendez, 2021)

Words to explain:

- Might impede students' comprehension when the teacher stops the read aloud to teach the word

- Not worth a great deal of instructional time or attention

- Easy to explain and move on with instruction

Keep the following points in mind when deciding whether you should teach or simply explain a word in a read aloud.

- Choose depth over breadth. Even once you've differentiated the words to teach from the words to explain, there can still be too many unfamiliar words! There's no magic number for the correct number of words to teach; instead, there is a significant variation with vocabulary instructional practices (Wasik et al., 2016). Because your intent is to provide meaningful interaction with novel words, focus on a select number of words and teach them deeply as opposed to briefly covering them. In a storybook of typical length, select four to six words to teach. These criteria help guide the selection of words to teach (Beck et al., 2013).

    - Words repeated more than once in a text

    - Words that are interesting and relevant to students in their everyday interactions (This is where teachers' knowledge of their students, home lives, and realities is essential. A fourth-grade teacher working with students living in high-rises in the South Bronx might select different words than a fourth-grade teacher in rural Maine—even when they read aloud from the same book!)

    - Words that relate to something students already know, as demonstrated in schemata theory (Use your precious instructional time to make new vocabulary acquisition stick to something your students have basic familiarity with.)

- Explain through simple, straightforward, student-friendly definitions (see figure 1.3). During a read aloud, don't send your students to the dictionary or lead students in using context clues to deduce meanings. Instead, give them a student-friendly definition of the word, which explains the word concisely and in everyday language. Adhere to the rule of *three Ss*: short, simple, and straightforward. This is not a time for multiple explanations of vocabulary words, grammatical reminders about parts of speech, or minilessons in word study or

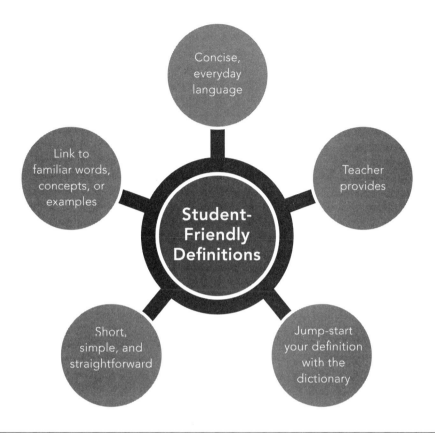

Figure 1.3: Key elements in student-friendly word definitions.

etymology. Because students are more likely to understand novel words if they've got foundational knowledge of a related word, teachers should often restate related words.

Here are some examples of specific things you might say to define words for students. Take the word *miserable*, for example. Say, "Miserable is another word for unhappy. If you feel miserable, you feel awful or sad." For *notice*, explain, "Notice is when you see something. Notice means to observe or watch."

Explain Through Think Alouds

Just as teaching or explaining new vocabulary is an important part of fostering student comprehension during read alouds, so is modeling for students ways to think about or ponder the meaning of texts. I have long believed in the power of *think alouds* or when proficient readers use first-person narrative *I language* to model their thinking (Ness, 2018). When I was a doctoral student doing clinical work with struggling readers, I found myself in a quandary: I had multiple data sources (observational measures, scores from norm-referenced assessments, and so on) indicating my students struggled to comprehend text, yet during tutoring time or classroom instruction, I found myself asking them questions that merely *checked* their understanding; questions like, "Where did the boy go next?" or "Why did the character leave the playground?" Eventually, I realized my well-intentioned efforts were somewhat pointless if my real aim was to *improve* students' understanding. So I embarked on what has become a lifelong love affair with think alouds.

Research confirms I was not alone in providing minimal comprehension instruction. Researcher Delores Durkin's (1978) milestone study shows less than 5 percent of instructional time in elementary classrooms consists of explicit comprehension instruction. My research since then shows minor increases in the frequency of explicit reading comprehension instruction; however, a very minor percentage of classroom instruction focuses on teacher modeling, explanation, application, and transfer of comprehension skills and strategies (Ness, 2011, 2016).

A wide body of research shows the effectiveness of think alouds in increasing reading comprehension (Ness, 2018; Pratt & Hodges, 2022). While conducting think alouds for a science text with kindergartners, education researchers Evan Ortlieb and Megan Norris (2012) report students who received think aloud instruction outperformed their peers in the control group on reading comprehension scores. Think alouds are effective for students of all ages, from preschool (Dorl, 2007) to secondary levels (Coiro, 2011; Lapp, Fisher, & Grant, 2008). Think aloud instruction benefits students across text format and genre: in online text (Coiro, 2011; Kymes, 2005), in narrative text (Dymock, 2007), and in informational text (Coiro, 2011; Lapp et al., 2008; Ortlieb & Norris, 2012). Equally promising are the benefits of think alouds for struggling readers (Berkeley & Larsen, 2018) and English learners (Ghaith & Obeid, 2004; McKeown & Gentilucci, 2007).

Perhaps think alouds' impressive power to improve student reading comprehension lies in how its verbal modeling makes the invisible cognitive process of understanding visible to students; a think aloud is as if you've cracked open your brain to show students all the steps and maneuvers to take to build understanding (see figure 1.4). *Think alouds are short instructional bursts in which teachers stop periodically and reflect—aloud—on their thinking and understanding.* The ultimate goal of thinking aloud is to show students how to independently transfer these purposeful actions toward their own reading.

In addition to explaining vocabulary in your read aloud, use it to explain potential stumbling blocks, areas of confusion, and what you do to improve your understanding when you face a challenge. As you start to think about incorporating think alouds into a read aloud, ask yourself questions like the following.

- "Where are the points of confusion for students? Where is their comprehension likely to unravel?"

- "Where might I incorporate think alouds to model understanding and improve student comprehension?"

Because think alouds fall under the teacher modeling realm of the instructional sequence, they should all begin with *I language.* Educators and researchers Douglas Fisher, Nancy Frey, and John Hattie (2017) explain that this first-person narrative activates "the ability—some call it an instinct—of humans to learn by imitation" (p. 58). Here are some sentence starters to use during think alouds.

- I'm confused here because . . .

- I'm getting the sense that . . .

- I'm wondering . . .

- Before I read, I thought . . . . Now I'm thinking . . .

- This makes me think . . .

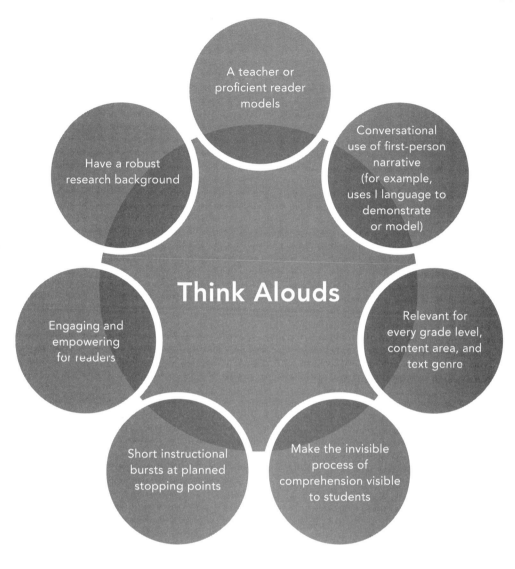

Figure 1.4: Defining think alouds.

- Now I understand . . .

- This information makes me think . . .

- The details I need to remember are . . .

The overarching purpose in the second step of planning is to proactively identify the problematic places in your read aloud, primarily unfamiliar vocabulary and comprehension roadblocks. Once you've identified these, you can head off any potential confusion by preteaching vocabulary and using think alouds to build comprehension.

At this stage in the process, you are again ready to put your thinking into context (as you did at the end of the evaluate step) and start filling out the Explain section of the read aloud planning template.

Explicitly identify vocabulary words and think alouds and add this information to the corresponding sections of the template (see figure 1.5, page 34).

Brainstorm Unfamiliar Words

This is simply a brain dump where you identify all the novel words in the text. In the subsequent columns, sort them more precisely.

Example:

Errand   Bawled   Cautionary   Tale   Block   Realized   Replied   Fussy   Boneless

Words to Teach	Short, Simple, Straightforward Definitions	Words to Explain	Short, Simple, Straightforward Definitions
Use this column for the four to six words that are relevant, interesting, and purposeful for students.	If it's useful, jump-start your thinking by looking up the word in the dictionary—but use that definition to craft a student-friendly definition.	Use this portion for the words that might be confusing but are not worthy of further instruction.	Keep those explanations laser focused on how the author uses the word in the text. Short, concise, and then move on!
Errand	An <u>errand</u> is a job that you do.	Cautionary	<u>Cautionary</u> means someone is giving you a warning about something that might be a problem.
Bawled	<u>Bawled</u> is another way to say cried hard.	Tale	A <u>tale</u> is the same thing as a story.
		Block	A <u>block</u> is how to measure distances in cities.
		Realized	<u>Realized</u> is another way to say learned or discovered something.
		Replied	<u>Replied</u> means answered.
		Fussy	<u>Fussy</u> is acting unhappy or complaining.
		Boneless	<u>Boneless</u> means limp. Trixie is refusing to walk, so she's going boneless and not moving since she's so upset.

(The left sidebar label for this section is: **Explain**)

Think Alouds

Here brainstorm meaningful places in the text to identify where to stop and develop the first-person transcript of what to say.

Example:
When Trixie and her father begin their journey.

Stopping or Pausing Points	I Language
"down the block" (p. 2)	This clue tells me that Trixie lives in a city, where a block is used to measure distance.

Source: Willems, 2004.

Figure 1.5: How to use the read aloud planning template for the explain step.

Engage and Extend

Finally, after finishing the evaluate and explain steps of planning a read aloud, it is time to consider ways to engage students and extend their learning after the read aloud is over. In this step, your aim is to invite students—as readers, thinkers, and human beings—into conversation, reflection, and inquiry about the text. Plan for opportunities that extend their thinking, enhance their wonderings, and cement their new realizations and learning from the text. While the focus of the explain step is to build comprehension, the focus here is to enhance students' social-emotional connections, help students retain the content through extension activities, and create a classroom culture of literacy through connection and conversation.

In this final planning step, home in on three areas: (1) social-emotional learning engagement, (2) cross-curricular extensions, and (3) extensions to support further reading and writing. Touch on as many instances of these three as possible, but realize not every book offers all three. Sometimes, there isn't a cross-curricular extension, but instead there is more robust engagement in social-emotional learning. In the planning template, simply jot down opportunities to highlight any of the three focus areas. These serve as reminders of areas you can expand on—as time allows—in your instruction. I'll examine each of these areas further, first beginning with social-emotional learning engagement.

Consider Social-Emotional Learning Engagement

Social-emotional learning engagement borrows heavily from the foundational work on social-emotional learning from the Collaborative for Academic, Social, and Emotional Learning (CASEL, n.d.a), which defines *social-emotional learning* as:

> An integral part of education and human development. [Social-emotional learning] is the process through which all young people and adults acquire and apply the knowledge, skills, and attitudes to develop healthy identities, manage emotions and achieve personal and collective goals, feel and show empathy for others, establish and maintain supportive relationships, and make responsible and caring decisions. . . . [Social-emotional learning] can help address various forms of inequity and empower young people and adults to co-create thriving schools and contribute to safe, healthy, and just communities.

More specifically, CASEL (n.d.a) identifies the following five tenets as essential in building social-emotional learning.

1. Self-awareness
2. Self-management
3. Social awareness
4. Relationship skills
5. Responsible decision making

This list dovetails with the competencies and skills teachers hope to foster in students, so in planning your read aloud, aim to specifically connect to one or more of these tenets. As you peruse the text, be intentional in evoking the themes, actions, characters, or events which might tap into these CASEL (n.d.a) tenets. Much of your social-emotional learning engagement may come in scaffolding conversations in small and large groups to foster class discussions on a shared text. Here are some of the questions to ask yourself to reflect on social-emotional learning connections to the text.

- "What social-emotional learning opportunities does the text present?"
- "In what way might I connect the theme, action, characters, or events of this text to one or more of the CASEL (n.d.a) tenets?"
- "Where might I enhance students' abilities to relate or learn from this text about ideas of identity, relationships, care for each other, or community building?"

If you connect these questions to *Knuffle Bunny*, for example, be mindful that PreK and early elementary-aged students don't often have the self-awareness to control their intense emotions—like the anger and anxiety Trixie feels when she's lost her beloved stuffed animal. This text presents the opportunity to help these young readers identify the character's emotion and relate it to times when they felt similar sentiments.

Develop Cross-Curricular Extensions

For the third step, also think through the interdisciplinary extensions the text offers. Because teachers should endorse reading aloud across content areas, read alouds are more powerful when they explicitly help students connect a book to a related content area or domain of knowledge. After all, just because a read aloud occurs in the English language arts block does not mean you should limit the conversation about the book to that time slot. Thoughts from the works of researchers and writers like Daniel Willingham's "How Knowledge Helps" (2006) and Natalie Wexler's (2019) *The Knowledge Gap* are particularly helpful as they remind teachers that because of the profound importance of background knowledge, teaching any content area is actually improving students' comprehension and retention in reading.

However, don't assume students will naturally make these interdisciplinary connections; they so often tie ideas, strategies, and information solely to the time slot or subject area when the teacher presents them. It's the job of teachers to help students see how a book read in an English language arts class directly relates to the social studies content—even if that social studies content is presented at a different time or on a different day. I recall my students in sixth-grade social studies erupting with delight when I read a book about how ancient Egyptians used geometry to plan the pyramids and simple pulleys and levers to move heavy building material. They eagerly shouted out, "We've talked about that stuff in math and science with Mr. Liao!" Little did they know that this cross-curricular extension was deliberate; Mr. Liao—my team teacher—and I met weekly to discuss our content (mine in English language arts and social studies, and his in mathematics and science), so we might enhance these interdisciplinary opportunities.

The point here is not to create a *text set*—a collection of related texts organized on a topic, theme, concept, or idea. Instead, make organic connections, often with a lighter touch. For example, as I read aloud from *Knuffle Bunny* (Willems, 2004), I do not go as far as to pull in maps to spotlight geography of city blocks or incorporate a washing machine manual to describe how laundromats work. Text set inclusion is engaging and impactful; in this instance, however, the aim is to spotlight those nuggets of knowledge students have because of another content area and excite them about learning across disciplines. After all, what's better than hearing students remark, "Hey, we've been talking about this same idea in [insert relevant content area]!" Here are some questions to ask yourself and reflect on as you think through cross-curricular extensions.

- "What text opportunities might I draw out to remind my students of cross-curricular connections?"

- "How might the events, characters, setting, plot, or theme of the text relate to different domains of knowledge?"

- "What are my students learning about in different content areas and how might I connect that learning to this text?"

- "With extra time, what might I showcase from this book to feature arts, music, social studies, mathematics, science, or English language arts?"

Ensure Extensions to Support Reading and Writing

After the last page is read aloud, a well-chosen book is ripe for literacy extensions. These *extensions* are the follow-up activities that help students process, retain, and extend the meaning of the text. Though here I use *reading and writing* as a label, all forms of literacy—including listening and speaking—are appropriate, particularly adapting for students' grade levels. For instance, a kindergarten extension might involve shared writing or the teacher acting as a scribe. The emphasis here, however, is *authentic extensions* to meaningfully build literacy skills. With every extension, ask yourself, "In what ways does this further my students as readers, writers, and thinkers?" If you can't answer these questions and connect your instruction to your teaching standards, you are merely planning a time-filling activity. For instance, although having students engage in an arts and crafts activity (where they build washing machines out of paper plates to depict Trixie's treasured stuffed animal among dirty clothes) might be cute, it's a bit of a stretch to connect it to authentic literacy. Your time would be better spent walking students through a graphic organizer highlighting setting, story elements, problem, and resolution. Here are some questions to ask yourself and reflect on as you seize additional literacy opportunities.

- "In what ways might I extend students' comprehension or retention of the text through reading and writing?"

- "What sorts of follow-up activities will enhance my students' knowledge of and connection with the text?"

- "How might writing, listening, or speaking help students better understand the text?"

- "What engaging and literacy-rich opportunities does this text offer after reading?"

There is a notion that teachers should follow up every read aloud with a graphic organizer, a written response, or an art project. But often, *conversation* is the most meaningful way for readers to connect to the text and one another in a culture of literacy. For example, take adult book clubs. Book clubs soared in popularity and frequency because their rich conversations connect readers through social interaction, enhanced by questions, reflection, debate, and analysis. Because oral language is the bedrock of literacy, be sure to include conversation as another level of engagement and extension, scaffolded through the questions in table 1.1 which are largely applicable across text genre, format, level, and content area. There are differentiated levels of questions—from simple to more complex— to meet the diverse needs of readers of different ages, levels, and backgrounds.

Table 1.1: Differentiated Levels of Questions

Simple	More Complex
How did this book make you feel?	What did you take away from this text? Were there any lessons, messages, or new information? What resonated with you?
What does this book remind you of?	
What did you learn from this book?	How has this book revised your thinking?
How did this book help grow your mind? How did it help grow your heart?	How has this book impacted how you feel?
	How are you different as a learner?
What jumped into your mind as you listened to this book?	How are you different as a person because of this book?
	How does this book connect to what you know in other subjects?
	In what ways does this book make you wonder or want to know more about . . . ?

Now that you've considered ways to further engage students with the text and to extend their learning after the read aloud, you're ready to complete the Evaluate section of the read aloud planning template. Once again, I use *Knuffle Bunny* (Willems, 2004) as an example (see figure 1.6). As a reminder, the content in the template is a brainstorm of *possibilities* to use with your students—not an agenda of exactly what to do. Further, be sure to prioritize the engage and extend elements most appropriate for your students. If a number of your students live in foster care, it might not be appropriate to have them conduct family interviews about their first words. As you'll see in figure 1.6, it's OK to have an unequal number of items for each portion of this step.

Social-Emotional Learning Engagement	Engage students in conversation with the following. *Examples:* • "Help me think of a word to describe how Trixie felt when she couldn't find Knuffle Bunny." • "Turn to a neighbor and share a time you felt like Trixie. How did your body feel? How did your heart and mind feel?" • "If you feel that way again, how might you handle the situation?"
Cross-Curricular Extensions	• Students map Trixie's neighborhood. • Students make maps of their own neighborhoods, noting the places they go when they run errands.
Extensions to Support Reading and Writing	• Character analysis: What does Trixie do, and how does she feel, see, and act? • Create fliers or wanted posters for Trixie's missing stuffed animal, including a written description. • Have students conduct an interview with parents or caregivers to recount their first word. • Generate a story of Knuffle Bunny's adventures written from Knuffle Bunny's perspective. "What happened and how did Knuffle Bunny feel when lost?"

Source: Willems, 2004.

Figure 1.6: How to use the read aloud planning template for the engage and extend step.

A Call to Action

Successful read alouds entail explicit preparation and planning. Move away from the notion that the first reading of a book should occur in front of students. My best read alouds have come from the times when I intentionally perused the text two, three, or four times.

In this section, I invite you to reflect on chapter content and on your own reading aloud practices. Use the following questions with a grade-level team, a co-teacher, or trusted colleagues. If you prefer your reflective process to be solitary, grab a pen—or keyboard—and write out your answers. Try to reflect without judgment—in other words, simply notice and don't label. For example, if you discover you don't typically plan your read alouds in advance, embrace this observation without a critical lens, but rather as an area for future direction or growth.

• Brainstorm the last five titles you read aloud. What patterns do you notice—if any—about your text selection?

• What makes you select a text for a read aloud? What key factors guide your text choices?

• Think through your last two weeks of instruction. How often did you read aloud? At what times of the day? During what content areas? Reflect on your comfort level with the duration and frequency of your read alouds. Did it feel too much? Too little? Brainstorm any times of the day you might use for read alouds.

• What is your typical preparation for a read aloud? Notice any areas where you might improve your read aloud preparation.

- What do you typically do before, during, and after your read aloud?

- How do you invite students into your read aloud? How do they connect with the book and converse about it?

- What is your favorite thing about reading aloud? Your least favorite?

- What resonates with you as you peruse the read aloud planning template? What opportunities do you notice? What challenges do you anticipate?

CHAPTER 2

Apply the Read Aloud Plan to Diverse Texts

Now that I've explained planning a read aloud and given some examples of how you can use the three-step process, I'll apply that process to three different engaging picture book texts for three different student age groups: PreK–2, 3–5, and 6–8. My use of picture books for all grade levels is deliberate. I did this because I wanted to select short enough texts to model the planning process in its entirety, and because I believe teachers can use picture books effectively for all students, including those in middle school (Costello & Kolodziej, 2006). As author Patricia Murphy (2009) explains, picture books are short enough to cover in their entirety, students generally enjoy them, and they provide engaging material in an accessible manner. Conceptually, picture book subjects range widely, and finding age-appropriate material for students in grades PreK–8 is an easy task.

Although the following examples are from picture books, you can apply this process across text format and genre.

Specifically, in this chapter, I will examine the following three texts.

- **Grades PreK–2 example:** *The Sandwich Swap* by Her Majesty Queen Rania Al Abdullah (2010)

- **Grades 3–5 example:** *Love in the Library* by Maggie Tokuda-Hall (2022)

- **Grades 6–8 example**: *The Secret Garden of George Washington Carver* by Gene Barretta (2020).

I will apply each step in the three-step planning process to each text and will end the discussion of each text by applying the entire planning process to the read aloud planning template. After the examination of the three texts, this chapter concludes with the repeating A Call to Action section with questions for reflection on chapter content. Take note that the following plans are purposefully very explicit. I've deliberately presented an entire menu of instructional options to act almost like training wheels. Just as adults support novice bike riders with training wheels so they gain the confidence and skill to ride without them, my hope is that the painstaking detail I provide here demonstrates a process—with the intent of eventually removing the "training wheels." Realistically, no teacher has the time to devote to such detailed planning for every read aloud—especially since read alouds should be a daily habit. While this process may seem time-consuming at first, I hope to demonstrate the planning process in its entirety to build your confidence in the process. The more exposure you have to the process, the more natural and inherent it will become.

Grades PreK–2 Example

The Sandwich Swap (Her Majesty Queen Rania Al Abdullah, 2010) is not new, but it has risen to the top of my list of favorites for PreK–2 students. This story appears relatively simple on the surface, but it offers important messages about friendship, acceptance, and understanding. The book opens with the mysterious, "It all began with a peanut butter and jelly sandwich" (Her Majesty Queen Rania Al Abdullah, 2010, p. 1), leaving the reader to wonder what is meant by the ambiguous *it*. Next, the reader meets Salma and Lily, two early elementary school-aged girls, who are immediately identified as best friends at school. The basis of their friendship is their shared interests: drawing, outdoor play and games, and lunchtime together. Conflict arises at lunch when each of the girls is secretly horrified by her friend's meal. Not only does Lily enjoy her peanut butter and jelly sandwich but it also reminds her of her father, who prepares it for her each day; Salma equally enjoys her hummus and pita sandwich and how it reminds her of her mother making it for her. Usually, the girls resist the urge to negatively comment about each other's lunches, until one day when they can no longer control their unkind thoughts. Lily tells Salma that her sandwich looks yucky; Salma responds by saying that Lily's sandwich smells gross. With hurt feelings, the girls avoid each other, until the next day in the school cafeteria when the entire class becomes embroiled in the conflict—hurling insults at one another and eventually escalating into a food fight. Ashamed that their disagreement was the root of such chaos, Salma and Lily help clean up the mess and are called into the principal's office. The following day, Salma and Lily nibble silently on their sandwiches, until Lily is courageous enough to offer Salma a bite of hers. The two swap sandwiches and are surprised by how much they enjoy each other's. They giggle and hug, and then report again to the principal's office to "suggest a very special event for the whole school" (Her Majesty Queen Rania Al Abdullah, 2010, p. 26). An illustration on a wordless full-page spread shows the class of children in front of a long table full of food. In front of each dish is a small flag, and the students appear to be serving each other and sampling from their neighbors' platters, while a group of adults looks on in the background. Lily and Salma are at the head of the table, and the final page of the book returns full circle to the opening pages with "And that's how it . . . ended with a hummus and pita sandwich" (Her Majesty Queen Rania Al Abdullah, 2010, p. 28).

I return to this book time and time again because it offers so many opportunities for social-emotional learning, conversations about friendship and diversity, nuances the reader must infer, and how much is packed into a relatively short text. Even though there are some references in the book that have not withstood the test of time, its message of friendship, forgiveness, and embracing differences are timeless. In the following section, I will walk through the text to evaluate it for the challenges and opportunities it presents for a read aloud.

Evaluate

The aim is to evaluate the text for potential stumbling blocks as well as opportunities, and also to specifically consider funds of knowledge and background knowledge students need to access this text. I wouldn't be so audacious as to bring food to class—due to pervasive food allergies and school policies—but I'd be sure to open up a conversation about what sandwiches and wraps are, and more generally, about what different kinds of foods people eat for lunch. I'd use my personal knowledge of my students to determine their familiarity with sandwiches. My former students in Oakland, California never brought sandwiches for lunch, but sandwiches were the lunch of choice at my daughter's elementary school in New York. Though I'd expect many students to understand peanut butter, hummus (a chickpea-based spread common in Middle Eastern dishes) might be less familiar.

Also be aware of the culture nuances that may be relevant to students. Remember from chapter 1 (page 17) that while background knowledge and funds of knowledge are similar categories that overlap, they differ as well, and funds of knowledge include those important cultural elements students learn not in school but in their homes and communities. This is where teachers' knowledge of their students is so pivotal. For instance, a school that serves an entire Title I population might be unfamiliar with the norms of students bringing lunches to school, as those students secure their lunches—and often breakfasts—at school. Further, the practice of sharing food might be unfamiliar to students. While my childhood lunchtime memories include swapping fruit roll-ups for snack cakes, some schools may strictly forbid food trading due to health, safety, religious, or cultural precautions.

While *The Sandwich Swap* (Her Majesty Queen Rania Al Abdullah, 2010) is relatively straightforward, it does include some potential stumbling blocks—including that nebulous opening sentence, "It all began with a peanut butter and jelly sandwich" (Her Majesty Queen Rania Al Abdullah, 2010, p. 1). The sentence might intrigue readers, but the use of the vague pronoun *it* could also potentially confuse them. "What began with a sandwich?" students may ask. Furthermore, the book ends with a return to this vague pronoun, declaring, "And *that's* how it all began . . ." (Her Majesty Queen Rania Al Abdullah, 2010, p. 28). Food fights might also confuse young readers (hopefully, they've not encountered any firsthand!). Another point of uncertainty might arise when a seemingly private disagreement between the story's main characters later unnecessarily involves the entire class. When Salma and Lily meet with the principal, the authors intentionally omit what the principal says—this sets the stage for a later inference readers must make and could potentially be a sticky spot for them. One of the book's loveliest nuances comes when the two girls reconcile their differences without any adult intervention, discipline, or even words of apology; I like to think the authors offer this as a reminder of keeping a sense of perspective about relatively minor tiffs. But this independent reconciliation could potentially confuse students. Finally, the book's full-page spread depicting a class picnic with foods from students' families is potentially confusing for students, as it appears with no accompanying text and requires visual literacy and inferencing skills. The more you can identify these potential sources of confusion in your planning, the more you'll be able to design instruction to circumvent comprehension breakdowns.

Explain

Now's the time to delineate the vocabulary words to briefly explain (words to explain) versus words worthy of instructional focus (words to teach). One word of importance in this story is *ashamed*, which is mentioned more than once and has obvious links to future social-emotional learning engagement, so I'm sure to provide instruction on this sophisticated and important word. Because some of the adjectives in the book—*splattered*, *icky*, *gooey*—describe both the setting and the sandwiches, teachers can easily explain them and do not necessarily warrant in-depth instruction.

When it comes to thinking aloud, *The Sandwich Swap* (Her Majesty Queen Rania Al Abdullah, 2010) is ripe for showcasing inferences. Take some of the potential confusing spots (mentioned previously) and be sure to think aloud about them to model how to address those instances when student comprehension breaks down. Also, this book carries a theme about acceptance and diversity that can make an important impact on readers, so highlight this in a think aloud to incorporate the author's purpose.

Engage and Extend

The Sandwich Swap (Her Majesty Queen Rania Al Abdullah, 2010) is replete with social-emotional learning opportunities, primarily those of self-awareness and relationship skills. This book offers plenty of opportunities to highlight *empathy*, as teachers engage students in questions that put them in similar predicaments. Salma and Lily demonstrate compassion as they resolve their conflict peacefully. There is also a wide range of emotions displayed in this book: *sadness*, *embarrassment*, and *happiness*. Teachers might engage readers in conversations about ways to resolve differences and show forgiveness. Be certain to engage students in a conversation about polite ways to express differences of opinion. For example, offer students language prompts like, "I'm not sure I agree with you" or "I have a different opinion, but . . . ." In a post-reading activity for PreK–2 students, you might use hand puppets to try out this language. Have students reenact Salma and Lily's difference of opinion in softer, kinder language.

Further, there are multiple ways to invite readers to connect this book to other content areas and support their comprehension through literacy extensions. A logical extension might highlight the importance of food as a part of one's family or culture, so students might begin with a writing prompt. If students are not yet writing independently, they might sketch a picture of the food and have an adult act as a scribe. Because literacy skills also center on oral language, students might practice question generation—as well as the give-and-take of conversation—with a partner or others, during which they explain the role of food in their home lives. To do this, pair students and give student A the prompt, "Tell me about a food that is special to your family," while student B builds oral language and works on syntax and sentence structure with the sentence frame, "The food special to my family is . . . ." Then have the students switch roles. These interviews might be especially useful for multilingual learners.

Figure 2.1 collates the three planning steps for *The Sandwich Swap* (Her Majesty Queen Rania Al Abdullah & DiPucchio, 2010). As a reminder, this planning template offers a menu of options, rather than a lockstep script.

Title of Text: *The Sandwich Swap* by Her Magesty Queen Rania Al Abdullah and Kelly DiPucchio (2010)

<table>
<tr><td rowspan="4">Evaluate</td><td colspan="4">

Background Knowledge

- Peanut butter and jelly sandwiches
- Hummus
- Outdoor activities, like jump rope

</td></tr>
<tr><td colspan="4">

Funds of Knowledge

- Food sharing as a symbol of friendship
- Bringing lunches to school, rather than eating school-provided lunches
- What a food fight is

</td></tr>
<tr><td colspan="4">

Potential Stumbling Blocks

- Vague pronoun on page 1
- Why other students get involved in disagreement
- No direct mention of what the principal tells Salma and Lily
- How Salma and Lily make up
- Final illustration depicting classwide picnic

</td></tr>
<tr><td colspan="4">

Instructional Opportunities

- Inferring to deduce what the final double-page illustration might be
- Allowing students to predict what the principal might have said to Salma and Lily
- Using illustrations to read the text, building visual literacy

</td></tr>
</table>

Brainstorm Unfamiliar Words

pesky scowled insults ashamed icky gooey blurted splattered rowdy

	Words to Teach	Short, Simple, Straightforward Definitions	Words to Explain	Short, Simple, Straightforward Definitions
Explain	pesky	Another word for annoying, describes something that causes trouble	icky	Another word for gross
			gooey	A thick, slimy texture
	scowled	When you make an unhappy face	blurted	When someone says something very quickly, without waiting
	insults	Unkind words someone says to someone else	splattered	Describes when there are drops of something all over
	ashamed	A feeling when you are not proud of how you acted; or you feel bad about something you did; similar to the feeling of embarrassment	rowdy	Very noisy

---

Figure 2.1: Completed read aloud planning template for *The Sandwich Swap* (Her Majesty Queen Rania Al Abdullah & DiPucchio, 2010).

continued ▶

Think Alouds

Salma and Lily eating together. When the girls first criticize each other's sandwich. When they start eating at separate tables. When the girls feel shame, help clean up the mess.

	Stopping or Pausing Points	I Language
Explain	"It all began with a peanut butter and jelly sandwich" (p. 1), and "it ended with a hummus sandwich" (p. 26).	"I want to know what *it* is. What began with a peanut butter sandwich? What ended with a hummus sandwich?"
	Salma and Lily eat their lunches together on page 13	"The key information: Salma and Lily are friends who have a lot in common."
	When the book tells us that Salma felt bad that her friend had to eat peanut butter, and in her mind calls the peanut butter gross on page 15	"I'm noticing the author wrote these two parts—about what Salma ate and thought, and what Lily ate and thought—in the exact same way. I wonder if the author did this to show me that even though the girls have so much in common, they also have things that are different."
	"'Your sandwich looks kind of yucky,' she blurted out" (p. 16).	"I'm noticing some words that don't always mean nice things—*pesky, yucky, blurted*. These words make me think Lily was acting unkindly."
	When Salma thinks about how her mother cuts her hummus sandwich in half each morning on page 16	"From the text clues, I get the sense that the hummus sandwich reminds Salma of home and of how much her mother loves her."
	On page 17 when Lily thinks of her father cutting her sandwich in triangles in the morning	"I'm noticing the sandwich reminds Lily of how much her dad loves her, just like Salma's sandwich reminds her that her mom loves her."
	"Salma ate her lunch at one table and Lily ate her lunch at another" (p. 19).	"Now I understand these friends are so hurt they don't spend time together like they normally do."
	When both girls feel ashamed on page 21	"I'm getting the sense Lily and Salma feel responsible for the food fight and the conflict with their classmates."
	After Salma and Lily help clean up the mess on page 22	"I'm wondering how the principal will handle this. Will Lily and Salma get in trouble? What will their punishment be? Did the principal call their parents? Did other students have to help clean up too?"
	When the girls laugh, hug, and exchange sandwiches on page 24	"I'm noticing the girls didn't apologize to each other. They just tried each other's lunch and realized how much they liked the other's. I wonder why the author doesn't write about apologies."
	". . . and ended with a hummus and pita sandwich" (p. 28).	"I can see from the pictures the entire class has a picnic where all students try different kinds of food and learn about others' families and cultures. I'm thinking the author wrote this book to make us realize that friends can have lots of things in common, but differences are not a bad thing."

<table>
<tr><td rowspan="4" style="writing-mode: vertical-rl;">Engage and Extend</td><td>

Social-Emotional Learning Engagement

Possible conversation starters:

- How did Salma and Lily resolve their differences?
- How did they work together to create something for everyone?
- How might things have been different had they respected each other's opinions and differences from the beginning?
- What might you do if your friend hurts your feelings? What might you do if you hurt your friend's feelings?
- How might you feel if someone said something unkind about something you loved? What might you say to that person?

</td></tr>
<tr><td>

Cross-Curricular Extensions

Mathematics:
- Write recipes for familiar foods and use fractions to increase the recipe (for example, if you need $\frac{1}{2}$ a tablespoon for one peanut butter sandwich, how much would you need for six sandwiches?)

Social Studies:
- Investigate chickpeas (where they are grown, what cultures eat them, and so on)
- Look into the history of the peanut butter sandwich and peanuts

Science:
- Investigate the climates necessary to grow chickpeas and peanuts

</td></tr>
<tr><td>

Extensions to Support Reading and Writing

- Have students interview loved ones about a food that reminds them of their home.
- Have students write or orally craft an apology to the principal, imagining what Salma and Lily might have said.
- Have students write or describe their favorite food from their family and culture.
- Have students write a detailed instruction booklet on how to make a peanut butter and jelly sandwich or a hummus and pita or wrap-style sandwich.

</td></tr>
</table>

Grades 3–5 Example

As a lifelong reader, I've long loved books about books, libraries, and reading culture. They somehow capture the magic of reading and the possibilities of books. I've also always gravitated toward stories about the human condition, and about how people overcome challenges and adversity to forge more optimistic paths. So when I came across the picture book *Love in the Library* (Tokuda-Hall, 2022), I snatched it up. This picture book—a true story about author Maggie Tokuda-Hall's (2022) maternal grandparents—tells the story of two teenagers who meet and fall in love while living in the brutality of a Japanese internment camp.

The book opens with Tama, a girl living in a Japanese internment camp nestled in the arid desert. She walks underneath the guard towers and barbed wire fence, avoiding eye contact with guards. Readers learn she has taken a job in the camp's library, though she has no formal library training. As she unlocks the library, she greets George, who is eagerly waiting for her. Tama and George have been in the Japanese internment camp—called *Minidoka*—for a year, although Tama should be graduating from college. Readers also learn the conditions at Minidoka are difficult year-round—with extreme heat and cold, crowding, and people of all ages losing the freedoms of their previous lives. The author explains that fear and anxiety are constants of the camps, yet George and his welcoming smile are also constants. Readers learn the library—and its books—provides an escape for Tama. When Tama and George sit across from each other in the library, she hushes him to remind him of the library rules. George asks Tama how she's feeling, and she explains her mix of emotions: fear, sadness, loneliness, hopefulness. Yet, she struggles to find a singular word that makes up this mix of emotions; George tells her the word *human* encompasses the complexity of her feelings. They reach for each other's hands across the table and smile, leaving Tama a bit less lonely. Tama finds out the reason George has been making daily trips to the library is not merely for the books but also to see her. Tama and George fall in love, marry, and have their first-born son in Minidoka. This book is ideal for upper-elementary (grades 3–5) students because of the opportunity to understand the time, setting, and context that drives the action, and the complex range of emotions the central characters feel.

Evaluate

A successful read aloud of *Love in the Library* (Tokuda-Hall, 2022) is highly dependent on careful preparation of students' background knowledge. To understand the setting, conflict, and character development, students must understand the American fear that arose after the 1941 bombing of Pearl Harbor. Two months after the bombing, President Franklin D. Roosevelt issued executive order 9066, which created military zones in western states (California, Washington, and Oregon) with significant Japanese American populations. This order aimed to prevent espionage. Initially these camps were voluntary, but eventually 120,000 Americans of Japanese ancestry were forcibly removed from their homes. If students have minimal background knowledge on this event and time period, you might use audiovisual support to show pictures or videos of the conditions of these prison camps. In addition to this background knowledge, there are social nuances—Tama's blushing, George's eager grin in Tama's direction, his waiting for her at the door of library—in the book that help students understand the budding romance between Tama and George. These funds of knowledge—as well as the notion of books as an escape from reality—are worthy of front-loading prior to reading.

In addition to the social-emotional learning opportunities, this book is a must-add to any coverage of World War II. There is ample material to engage students in character analysis of Tama. *Love in the Library* (Tokuda-Hall, 2022) is a stellar example of a text about characters from underrepresented or marginalized groups in which the author shares the same identity. The author's own experiences with her grandparents inspire the writing, which is done from their perspective.

Explain

One of the book's most compelling elements is its emotional undercurrent; to clarify this for students, use your think aloud to intentionally elucidate Tama's feelings. You also want your students to understand the impact the trauma inherent in the setting of the prison camp has on Tama, so be sure to verbalize that here. In a lovely scene where Tama struggles with her breadth of conflicting emotions, George notes that she is *human*. This use of figurative language is worthy of exploration. George does not mean Tama is literally a human being (that is, a Homo sapien), but rather he is validating her emotional complexity. To help students understand this nuance, offer a think aloud here.

From the ample vocabulary words in *Love in the Library* (Tokuda-Hall, 2022), purposefully select the words repeated in the text—such as *miracle* and *constant*. Also, intentionally provide instruction for the word *unjust*, as this word resonates with the book's theme.

Engage and Extend

CASEL's (n.d.a) principle of *social justice*—the ability to understand the perspectives of and empathize with others—resonates throughout this text. A specific aim might be for students to feel compassion for Tama and George, and anger that they are interned because of their culture. So students will become invested in the budding love story between Tama and George. I hope students show concern for the characters and admire their resilience in their unjust imprisonment.

To help guide literacy extensions, it's important to consider the context for using *Love in the Library* (Tokuda-Hall, 2022). For instance, a middle school social studies teacher using the text in a larger unit on World War II might have students read journal entries—to explore primary documents—from those living in Japanese internment camps. Whereas a fourth-grade teacher using the same text to explore the impact of books and libraries on learning and development might have students generate poetry about how books make them feel. To cover the wide range of literacy opportunities, focus on fostering students' social-emotional connections to the text, as well as enhancing students' understanding of this historical period, its impact, and evaluating the justness of the characters' treatment.

Figure 2.2 (page 50) offers a delineated menu of my instructional approach for *Love in the Library* (Tokuda-Hall, 2022) in the read aloud planning template.

Title of Text: *Love in the Library* by Maggie Tokuda-Hall (2022)

<table>
<tr><td rowspan="4">Evaluate</td><td>

Background Knowledge

- What a desert is
- The setup of prisons (guard towers, barbed wire fences)
- What a library is and the role of a librarian
- Japanese internment camps established during World War II
- College and graduation
- The location of the West Coast of the United States
- A general overview of baseball and its popularity with Japanese Americans

</td></tr>
<tr><td>

Funds of Knowledge

- Why people avoid eye contact
- How people feel in crowded spaces, and what it feels like to not have privacy
- The stress of constant fear and anxiety
- A love of books and the escapism books and reading provide
- Why people blush
- Libraries as quiet places where people speak in hushed volumes

</td></tr>
<tr><td>

Potential Stumbling Blocks

- Without sufficient preteaching about Japanese internment camps, this setting will be problematic. Without understanding how the setting influences the characters, readers will not fully grasp the conflict.
- The figurative use of the word *human*
- There is a jump in timeline—the majority of the story occurs in the prison camp, but the author fast-forwards the time frame at the end of the book.

</td></tr>
<tr><td>

Instructional Opportunities

- Chances for rich character analysis
- Focus on an often-overlooked event in American history
- Provides inside perspective from voices not amplified historically

</td></tr>
</table>

Brainstorm Unfamiliar Words

elderly   frustrated   unjust   constant   miracle or miraculous   latrine   replied   uncomfortable   grinning   focus   complain   privacy

Words to Teach	Short, Simple, Straightforward Definitions	Words to Explain	Short, Simple, Straightforward Definitions
elderly	Describes someone who is old	latrine	An outdoor toilet
frustrated	Another word for angry	replied	Another way to say answered
unjust	Another word for unfair	uncomfortable	When something does not feel good
constant	When something does not change	grinning	Another way to say smiling
miracle or miraculous	Something unexpected and amazing happens (Miraculous is something that you didn't think would happen, but it's wonderful that it did.)	focus	The center of attention
		complain	When you say you're unhappy about something
		privacy	When you have no one's attention on you

(Explain)

Explain	**Think Alouds** The narrator explaining how Tama feels and responds to her surroundings, the narrator describing the camp, the introduction of George, and so on.	
	Stopping or Pausing Points	**I Language**
	When the narrator explains that Tama doesn't like the desert and avoids looking at the guards on page 1	"I'm getting the sense Tama is in some sort of prison in the desert—it's hot, dry, and dusty, and there are fences and guards watching her. It doesn't sound like a great place to be."
	"People did jobs that needed doing, and that was that" (p. 3).	"The word *camps* combined with the guards and the fences reminds me that the setting of the book is a camp. Not a summer camp where kids go for fun, but a place where people are held in one place or because they are in trouble or can't leave."
	". . . and then followed her inside" (p. 4).	"The author really wants me to understand George loves the library. He gets there before it even opens, and he takes out a stack of books every day."
	". . . uncomfortable and unjust" (p. 5).	"It's confusing to me how something can be both different and the same, but I think the author is trying to show me how unfair it was to lock up a group of people in a prison camp just because they all have the same background. All of the people in Minidoka are Japanese American, like Tama."
	"No one had any privacy" (p. 8).	"The author is reminding me how difficult it was to be in this camp, with harsh weather and everyone having to share everything."
	"Constant questions. Constant worries. Constant fear" (p. 11).	"I'm getting the sense it wasn't just hard to live in these camps (because of the weather and not having privacy) but also because Tama was not sure if her life would ever go back to how it used to be. Now, she's always scared and worried."
	". . . George and his big smile were constant" (p. 12).	"It sounds to me like George is the best part of Tama's day—with his smile and always being at the library."
	When the narrator mentions that the library, even though it is small, fits so much inside on page 14	"So constant can be both good and bad! Here the library—filled with books that let Tama imagine she were somewhere else—is a good kind of constant. I'm getting the sense this library and the books were an escape for Tama."
	"But she could not make herself smile" (p. 18).	"I'm wondering why Tama seems so down. One thing I notice about her is that she finds the good in every situation. Another word for that is *optimistic*. But now, she can't even find a smile. Something must really feel wrong."
	When the narrator tells us Tama is crying on page 20	"The author really wants me to understand how many big feelings Tama is having about living in this prison camp, and that George understands, probably because he feels them too."

Figure 2.2: Completed read aloud planning template for *Love in the Library* (Tokuda-Hall, 2022).

continued ▶

Explain	When the narrator tells us how Tama feels after George says the word human on page 22	"I'm not sure I understand what George means when he says *human*. I don't think the author means that Tama is human because she's a person, but I think the author is using *human* here to describe how people feel so many different things at once. George is reassuring Tama it's OK to have a lot of different feelings and emotions."
	"It was her, Tama" (p. 24).	"Now I understand George wasn't visiting the library every day because he loved books, but rather, he loved Tama!"
	"But it is in all of us" (p. 30).	"I'm getting the sense the author wrote this book as a reminder that beautiful things can come out of hardship—like love coming out of a prison camp. I'm thinking the miracle is to stay positive and focus on the good, even when times are difficult."

Engage and Extend

Social-Emotional Learning Engagement

Possible conversation starters:

- What emotions do you see Tama express in the book? What about George?
- How did you feel when you found out about the Japanese internment camps?
- How does Tama display strength in the book?
- Analyze this sentence. What do you think the author means here? "But to fall in love in a place like Minidoka, a place built to make people feel like they weren't human—that was miraculous. That was humans doing what humans do best" (p. 28).
- Talk about a time when you've felt a mix of emotions.
- What do you think is unjust in the world today? Describe your reaction to that injustice.
- Have you—or a friend—experienced a miracle? How did it feel?

Cross-Curricular Extensions

Social Studies:
- Conduct research on Japanese internment camps
- Explore primary sources—journals, letters, records—from internment camps
- Connect Japanese internment camps to other historical instances of discrimination due to heritage

Mathematics:
- Chart or graph the number of Japanese American citizens housed in internment camps

Science:
- Investigate the desert biome—its climate, topography, geography, and so on

Fine Arts:
- Explore *The Art of Gaman* (Hirasuna, 2005)—the arts and crafts made by Japanese Americans in U.S. internment camps during World War II
- View the works of noteworthy Japanese artists who created during this time period (for example, Ruth Asawa, Tsutomu "Jimmy" Mirikitani, Isamu Noguchi, Henry Sugimoto, and master woodworkers Gentaro and Shinzaburo Nishiura)
- Research how music and dance thrived in prison camps
- Follow up with the picture book *A Place Where Sunflowers Grow* by Amy Lee-Tai (2006), which tells about a child's art class in the internment camps

Physical Education:
- Notice the sport that takes place in Minidoka. Explore "Baseball and Barbed Wire" from the nonprofit American Innings (https://americaninnings.org). Why was baseball so important in places like Minidoka? Follow up with these picture books:
  - *Barbed Wire Baseball: How One Man Brought Hope to the Japanese Internment Camps of WWII* by Marisa Moss (2013)
  - *Baseball Saved Us* by Ken Mochizuki (1993)

	Extensions to Support Reading and Writing

Engage and Extend	• Write journal entries from Tama's point of view.
	• Explore the letters compiled in the book *Write to Me: Letters From Japanese American Children to the Librarian They Left Behind* by Cynthia Grady (2018). Write a similar letter.
	• Complete graphic organizers with text-based evidence on the character traits Tama demonstrates.
	• Explore graphic novels depicting the realities of Japanese internment camps:
	   • *Stealing Home* by J. Torres (2021)
	   • *They Called Us Enemy* by George Takei, Justin Eisinger, and Steven Scott (2020)
	   • *Displacement* by Kiku Hughes (2020)

Grades 6–8 Example

Are you familiar with George Washington Carver? Maybe you've heard of him as an inventor and an agricultural scientist. Contrary to popular belief, Carver did not invent peanut butter—but he did find nearly three hundred uses for peanuts, including sauces, oils, cleaning products, drinks, and even medicine. In addition to being an inventor, Carver was a human rights advocate—promoting racial harmony in the segregated South and even traveling to India to discuss nutrition with Mahatma Gandhi.

Author Gene Barretta's (2020) *The Secret Garden of George Washington Carver* chronicles Carver's inspirational life and passion for service. Born into slavery in 1864, Carver, a self-driven learner, was fascinated by the natural world. Desperate to attend school—but denied because of his skin color—Carver created a secret garden as an escape. With careful attention to the needs of the plants and soil, he earned the nickname *Plant Doctor*. His unbounded curiosity led Carver to leave his farm home at the age of twelve in search of new adventure. For the next eighteen years he studied agriculture at several schools in different states—eventually enrolling as the first Black man at Iowa Agricultural College. Booker T. Washington hired Carver, who built a farming laboratory at Tuskegee Institute. Carver convinced farmers of the multifunctional properties of peanuts, eventually developing three hundred uses for them. As a result, peanuts became the largest crop in the South. Carver demonstrated a strong commitment to service and created a traveling schoolhouse, the *Jessup Agriculture Wagon*, which traveled the countryside to teach poor farmers about healthy living, medical care, and farm upkeep. Despite his many awards and accolades, Carver was known for his humility and respect for nature.

This biographical picture book offers many cross-curricular opportunities for middle school readers—with possible conversations about farming, agriculture, and climate change. *The Secret Garden of George Washington Carver* presents a noteworthy man who overcame adversity, embraced a life of service, and emerged as an early environmentalist and proponent of racial harmony (Barretta, 2020). The book's rich vocabulary and vivid illustrations of garden scenes make it an appealing read aloud for upper-elementary (grades 3–5) and middle school (grades 6–8) readers.

Evaluate

At the middle school level, it is likely most students will have had some instruction on racism and the United States' history of slavery and segregation. As these factors impact Carver's development, teachers should help students activate any preexisting relevant background knowledge. Additionally, the book includes references to U.S. Congress, and students will benefit from reminders and brief overviews of this legislative body and its roles.

It is highly likely students might be unfamiliar with *agriculture*—especially for those not living in rural communities. Although students might not be familiar with the term itself, they will likely have background knowledge on farming; however, it's highly likely the uses of peanuts (other than the familiar peanut butter) will be novel. As a hook prior to reading, you might have students brainstorm and research how peanuts are farmed and used for many functions.

Explain

This text offers many opportunities to examine how an individual and a situation change based on unfolding action. Multiple think alouds, particularly those that focus on synthesizing, reflect these opportunities. As you examine Carver's contribution to history and the obstacles he overcame, it's also important to model analyzing the author's purpose, as you'll see in forthcoming think alouds. Because a potential stumbling block is the jumping back and forth in Carver's life, be sure to elucidate this through think alouds. The book's vocabulary is fairly straightforward, but lends itself to rich descriptive language about the concepts of humility and racial harmony.

Engage and Extend

The book (and Carver as a historical figure) offers opportunities to examine CASEL's (n.d.b) *competency guidelines for responsible decision making*, which it defines as, "The abilities to make caring and constructive choices about personal behavior and social interactions across diverse situations." This competency includes evaluating one's actions for personal, social, and collective well-being. CASEL (n.d.b) includes the following qualities about responsible decision making:

- Demonstrating curiosity and open-mindedness
- Identifying solutions for personal and social problems
- Anticipating and evaluating the consequences of one's actions
- Reflecting on one's role to promote personal, family, and community well-being
- Evaluating personal, interpersonal, community, and institutional impacts

All these qualities are inherent in Carver, as he uses his lifelong learning and curiosity to help others, to use science to improve communities, and to educate those in need. Furthermore, Carver demonstrates notable self-awareness—another CASEL (n.d.b) competency—as shown through his humility, purpose, and integrity. Figure 2.3 uses the read aloud planning template to overview the planning process for this award-winning book.

Title of Text: *The Secret Garden of George Washington Carver* by Gene Barretta (2020)

Evaluate

Background Knowledge

- The role of Congress
- That a peanut is a plant
- Racism and segregation through the early 1900s
- Basic overview of plant life
- Life experiences for people who were enslaved during the Civil War era
- The end of slavery because of the Emancipation Proclamation

Funds of Knowledge

- How an audience behaves when a speaker captivates them
- Frugality and resourcefulness
- How to convey humility

Potential Stumbling Blocks

- Switching of time frame throughout the book—not a linear unfolding of Carver's life
- Lack of background knowledge or experience with agriculture

Instructional Opportunities

- Inclusion of direct quotes from the historical figure
- Text-based evidence to examine character traits
- Rich inclusion of metaphors and similes, and descriptive language to illustrate his garden

Explain

Brainstorm Unfamiliar Words

agriculture   humble   encouraged   transformed   generosity   experimented   environmentalist   segregated   foolish   chores   outlawed   denied   soil   nutrients

Words to Teach	Short, Simple, Straightforward Definitions	Words to Explain	Short, Simple, Straightforward Definitions
agriculture	The science of farming or plants	segregated	When people were treated differently because of who they were
humble	When you don't believe you are important or unduly proud	foolish	Describes something that is silly
encouraged	When you say something kind to someone or praise them	chores	Small jobs people have to do
transformed	Another way to say changed	outlawed	Something the law doesn't allow
generosity	When you are willing to give or share; comes from the word *generous*	denied	When you stop someone from doing something
experimented	When you tried things out to learn	soil	Another word for the dirt in a garden
environmentalist	Someone who cares deeply about the Earth or taking care of the environment	nutrients	A kind of vitamin

Figure 2.3: Completed read aloud planning template for *The Secret Garden of George Washington Carver* (Barretta, 2020).

continued ▶

Think Alouds

When Carver speaks to Congress. Perhaps pause several times for this because it is so important. Also pause a key moments in Carver's background story. Show how he relates to nature.

Stopping or Pausing Points	I Language
". . . Carver was not among friends" (p. 2).	"I'm wondering who Carver is and why he's speaking to the Congress? I know he's Black, and I also know in 1921—when the book tells me he's speaking—Black people were not treated equally. I think that's what the author means when he says, 'Carver was not among friends' (p. 2). I also want to know about why and how peanuts are valuable."
"He gave the audience ten minutes they would never forget" (p. 2).	"I'm thinking that in those ten minutes, Carver said something really important—my clue is 'ten minutes they would never forget.'" (p. 2).
"Carver spoke for over an hour" (p. 3).	"Two things changed in my thinking—first, I'm now seeing how valuable peanuts are! And I'm also seeing Carver's speech was impressive—at first they limited him to ten minutes and laughed at him, but now they let him speak as long as he wanted!"
When the narrator explains how Carver relates to elements of the natural world, such as the dandelions on page 6	"It's important for me to remember this part jumps back in time to when Carver was a child."
"'Don't let flowers take you away from your chores,' warned Moses and Susan Carver" (p. 7).	"The big idea here is people don't understand why Carver likes flowers and plants so much."
When the narrator tells us that Carver filled the house with things from outdoors on page 10	"The author really wants me to understand Carver did not have an easy childhood. He was enslaved on a farm without his mother, and he was quite sick as a child. It sounds like he began to explore nature to cope with these challenges."
"'I want to know the name of every stone and flower and insect and bird and beast,' he said" (p. 13).	"I'm getting the sense Carver learned about how useful plants can be from Susan. And his curiosity about plants makes him want to learn even more."
"And no matter how much people discouraged him, he wanted to grow flowers" (p. 14).	"An important thing for me to realize about Carver is how eager he is to learn. Even when he's not allowed to attend school, he thinks of nature as a classroom."
"It was a special garden and could have remained secret forever. But, eventually, the young boy's generosity changed that" (p. 20).	"I'm learning a lot here about Carver, in addition to seeing how eager he is to learn. I'm also seeing he's resourceful—so he finds a purpose for everything in nature like Susan taught him. I'm also recognizing the joy the garden brings to Carver. I see him as a sort of scientist—where he observes and experiments, and learns by trying things."
"'Here comes the Plant Doctor,' they'd say whenever he paid a visit" (p. 22).	"I'm seeing here Carver is using his knowledge of plants to help other people. I think that's what the author meant by *generosity*."
When Carver leaves home at age twelve on page 24	"The author really wants to remind me how curious Carver is about plants and the world, and how brave he is to leave home at such a young age."

Explain

Explain	"In 1896, George Washington Carver became the first Black man to study at, graduate from, and teach at Iowa Agricultural College" (p. 26).	"So I'm thinking Carver really took that advice—to learn everything and give it back to the people—to heart. He spent so many years learning, and eventually became a teacher, so he could give back that knowledge."
	When the narrator tells us that peanuts became the biggest crop on page 28	"The big idea here is peanuts are useful because they helped make the farms and soil better with their nutrients, but they were also useful in many different ways. Now I'm seeing you can do so much more with peanuts than just eat them."
	"The best time to plow or how to raise a strong cow" (p. 30).	"I'm noticing how dedicated Carver is to bringing knowledge to the people—wherever they are! He's generous in sharing the knowledge he knows poor farmers need."
	"Regard Nature. Revere Nature. Respect Nature" (p. 34).	"I'm thinking the author wrote this book not only to tell me about how important Carver was as an agriculturalist but also how he helped people across the world. The author wants me to see Carver was kind, humble, and generous with his knowledge, and a leader in conversations about race and with other world leaders. I'm also confirming that although so much changed in his life, one thing that was a constant was his garden."

Engage and Extend

Social-Emotional Learning Engagement

- Carver used his passion for plants and nature to help others. What are you passionate about and how can your passions help the world and other people?
- How did Carver's choices impact his community and the world?
- What are some ways you help others—including your family and your community?
- Discuss the racism Carver endured. In your opinion, do people still face racism today? How and where have you seen or experienced racism?

Cross-Curricular Extensions

Science:
- Conduct research on the plants named in the book, such as black-eyed Susans and dandelions
- Investigate the ways plants and gardens contribute to healthy environments
- Conduct experiments to understand the conditions for growing seeds (for example light, water, temperature, and so on)
- Study and diagram the life cycle of a seed
- Choose a flower or plant near your home to study and observe

Art:
- Without looking at the illustrations, read aloud the descriptions of Carver's secret garden as students draw their own interpretations or visualizations
- Use berries and flowers to make paint, just as Carver did

Social Studies:
- Make a timeline of Carver's life
- Listen to recordings of Carver's speech to Congress
- Research additional global leaders Carver met with
- Research the geographic areas where Carver lived

Extensions to Support Reading and Writing

- Discuss the similes and metaphors in the book, particularly those the author used when describing Carver's childhood garden.
- Locate additional speeches by Carver and analyze them to determine his message, interpret his use of language, and evaluate its effectiveness.

A Call to Action

In many ways, this chapter has been a sort of written think aloud. In other words, what I've tried to do here is fluidly (as opposed to more incrementally, as I did in chapter 1, page 17) model the steps teachers should go through as they plan read alouds for students in early childhood, elementary, and middle school classrooms. Just as teachers aim to be as explicit as possible in thinking aloud for students, I've purposefully written this chapter as if you were inside my head during the planning of three of my favorite books.

My hope is you are ready to take this process and apply it to a text of your choice. I encourage you to grab that book and some paper and walk through the process with these reflective questions to guide you. If you're not quite ready to try it solo, team up with a partner or grade-level colleagues. And throughout your planning, I encourage you to have this question at the back of your mind: "In what ways is this planning process different from what I previously did with my read alouds?" Here are additional questions to get your planning started.

- Why have you selected this particular book and how does it align with your learning standards or instructional objectives?

- What instructional opportunities does the book offer? What instructional obstacles does the book present?

- To be successful, what do students need to know about the content, character, setting, topic, and so on before the read aloud of this book?

- What unfamiliar vocabulary does the book introduce? What words can you simply explain and move on, and which are the words to teach, the ones you want your students to use in their everyday conversation and writing?

- How does the book relate to other learning topics in other books, content areas, classes, and previous instruction?

- How might you extend the ideas and content in the book across disciplines (mathematics, science, social studies, arts, music, and so on)?

- What other literacy opportunities does the book offer to enhance your students' reading, writing, speaking, and listening? What lessons or messages does the book offer about social-emotional development?

- How might the book bolster your students' progress toward the five CASEL (n.d.b) competencies?

CHAPTER 3

Use Age-Appropriate Read Aloud Strategies

Throughout this book, I've implored for the need for read alouds every day for students of every age or grade level. I'd like to start this chapter by revisiting the current trends that reveal how read alouds decline as students increase in age. A Scholastic (n.d.) report shows the following key trends.

- Of all surveyed teachers (grades PreK–12), 64 percent report reading aloud to students.

- Among elementary school teachers, 83 percent report reading aloud to students.

- Among middle school teachers, 53 percent report reading aloud to students.

- While 77 percent of teachers set time aside for independent reading or read aloud time, only 36 percent do this every school day. On average, students who engage in independent reading or read aloud time spend twenty-two minutes on this activity daily.

The purpose of this chapter is to provide strategies to make reading aloud doable for teachers and as rewarding as possible for all PreK–8 students. To this end, you will find five strategies to apply with your students. I've presented the strategies in chronological order by age level; however, some of these strategies can span multiple grade bands. Those strategies are as follows.

- **Early childhood strategy (grades PreK–2):** Draw attention to the print.

- **Early childhood strategy (grades PreK–2):** Encourage conversation about the text.

- **Elementary and middle school strategy (grades 3–8):** Don't show the pictures—at first.

- **Early childhood, elementary, and middle school strategy (grades PreK–8):** Jump-start student-generated questions.
- **Elementary and middle school strategy (grades 3–8):** Read from diverse text diets.

Notice some of these strategies target a particular age or grade group, while others cross grade levels. The chapter concludes with the repeating A Call to Action section and questions to use to reflect on chapter content.

Early Childhood Strategy (grades PreK–2): Draw Attention to the Print

Did you know young children (PreK and earliest elementary grades)—on average—spend only 5 percent of reading time looking at the printed text in a read aloud (Evans, Williamson, & Pursoo, 2008; Justice, Skibbe, Canning, & Lankford, 2005)? Studies using eye tracking reveal young children naturally gravitate toward illustrations and spend almost no time focusing on the words. And when they overlook the text itself, they miss opportunities to enhance their early literacy skill of print awareness. Research highlights the promising results of *print referencing*, a read aloud technique where educators explicitly draw attention to the words on the page; preschool students whom teachers read to with a print-referencing approach fixate on print twenty thousand times more often in only ten minutes a day (Justice, Pullen, & Pence, 2008). Print referencing includes four techniques to highlight the forms and functions of print (Zucker, Ward, & Justice, 2009).

1. "Questions" (p. 62; for example, ask, "Where do I start reading on this page?" and "Why do you think this word is in bold?")

2. "Requests" (p. 63; for example, say, "Show me where the title is on the cover" and "Point to a lowercase letter")

3. "Comments" (p. 63; for example, say, "The label on this box says . . . " and "I'm noticing two words on this page that are the same")

4. "Nonverbal techniques" (p. 63; for example, show how to track left-to-right print and how to point to individual words)

The use of these techniques increases young children's *metalinguistic awareness*—or their ability to focus attention on spoken and written language (Zucker et al., 2009).

Powerful in its simplicity, print referencing can be effective in any type of text read aloud for students in the earlier grades. It is important for learners to clearly see the text in print referencing, so use this strategy in small-group instruction or individual sessions. If using print referencing during a whole-group read aloud, big-format books ensure all learners can see exactly where the teacher is pointing; projecting pages through a document camera is a fine substitute.

For readers at beginner levels, or those unfamiliar with print conventions, you might begin with modeling (saying, for example, "I'm noticing this sentence has quotation marks, which let me know a character is speaking."). For more experienced readers, you might invite their participation (saying, "Can someone point out a question mark on this page?"). The following list outlines additional print features worthy of attention.

- Labels, including those associated with figures, diagrams, or photos
- Labeled objects (for example, stop signs, labels on food items in illustrations)
- Speech bubbles that indicate a character talking
- Font changes, including size, color, orientation, italics, or boldface

The following list (Zucker et al., 2009) overviews how to highlight five features in print referencing in an unfolding developmental progression (from least to most sophisticated skills).

1. Clarifying *print function* is an important foundational print feature to reference. You might explain to students that typefaces indicate meaning. You might say, for example, that words that appear a certain way indicate that a character is talking, or that the color or size of words suggest what the character feels (Zucker et al., 2009).

2. Making students aware of *environmental print* is very important. You might point out print within illustrations, such as signs, labels, and lists, for example. You might tell them, for instance, that a jar in a picture has the word *cookies* written on it. You might take the time to read the traffic signs in a picture book (Zucker et al., 2009).

3. Guiding students in *book organization* is a critical part of assisting in building comprehension skills. You might point out to students the order in which we read text across a page, using a finger sweep. You might show the different parts of the book, saying what the cover is, for instance, and discussing its function (Zucker et al., 2009).

4. Building *letter knowledge* with students helps them prepare to read. You might explain to students the purpose of letters and that as units they make up whole words. Give the names of letters. Tell them about the letters, that the little and big *S* look the same, for instance (Zucker et al., 2009).

5. Assisting in *word identification* is a crowning skill. You might discuss the varying lengths of words, discuss how they sound, and what letters make up a word (Zucker et al., 2009).

An advantage of print referencing is its ease of application during routine read alouds; it does not require significant advance preparation, and you can incorporate it in conjunction with any other read aloud routine. As Zucker and colleagues (2009) explain:

> Teachers must be strategic in considering how much attention to print should occur to promote children's learning about the forms and functions of print while not detracting from the reading experience or other benefits that might be gained from that experience. (p. 67)

Print referencing during read alouds reminds the PreK–2 grades readers to specifically pay attention to the print on the page, a behavior that does not typically occur independently. Additionally, when teachers incorporate print referencing—either through modeling or student involvement—students increase their knowledge of measures of print concepts, concept of word, and word identification (Lovelace & Stewart, 2007).

Early Childhood Strategy (grades PreK–2): Encourage Conversation About the Text

The typical read aloud can be quite teacher dominated (that is, the teacher often controls or contributes most of the language). While there are definite benefits to this pattern, teachers run the risk of the read aloud being a passive activity where students just observe and listen. To invite students to interact (through sharing the discourse and conversation) in the read aloud, introduce an oldie but a goodie: *dialogic reading*. Dialogic reading is an interactive book reading practice designed to enhance students' language output and involvement in a read aloud. Grover J. Whitehurst and colleagues (David S. Arnold, Jeffery N. Epstein, Andrea L. Angell, Megan Smith, & Janet E. Fischel; 1994) proposed that implementing the technique in the classroom encourages student-teacher conversation and discussion during read alouds. The goal in dialogic reading is to turn the text into a dialogue or conversation, where students co-construct language. In dialogic reading, the teacher facilitates the reading and the student becomes the storyteller; in this role reversal, the teacher acts as the audience while the student is actively involved in the read aloud. There's no real magic to this approach, other than basic interaction and engagement with the text, shared between teacher and students. A key component of the dialogic reading technique is the *PEER sequence* (Whitehurst et al., 1994). The PEER sequence fosters short, language-based interactions between the student and teacher in the following manner.

- **P**rompt the student to say something about the book.
- **E**valuate the student's response through praise and encouragement.
- **E**xpand the student's response by building on it, rephrasing it, and enhancing it with additional information.
- **R**epeat the initial prompt, encouraging the student to use any new information or words you provide.

Here's an example of using the PEER sequence with a text about flowers.

> Teacher: (Pointing to the petals in illustration) "What's this?"
>
> Student: "The petals."
>
> Teacher: "That's right. The petals of the flower are bright colors to attract insects. Tell me, why are flowers bright colors?"

Every page presents an opportunity to elicit conversation through dialogic reading. As leading researchers on dialogic reading, Whitehurst and colleagues (1994) provide five types of prompts, (use the mnemonic *CROWD* to jog your memory), as table 3.1 displays.

Here's another example of using dialogic reading with a well-known nursery rhyme, "Jack and Jill":

> Jack and Jill went up the hill
> To fetch a pail of water.
> Jack fell down
> And broke his crown
> And Jill came tumbling after.

Table 3.1: Five CROWD Prompts to Use in Dialogic Reading

	Type of Prompt	Explanation	Example
C	Completion	The teacher leaves a blank and encourages students to fill it in. Use mostly with rhyming texts or those with repetitive phrases.	"Brown bear, brown bear, what do you see? I see a _____ looking at me!" (Martin, 1970, p. 1)
R	Recall	The teacher questions students about a familiar book, which supports the students' understanding of text sequence and plot.	"Can you tell me what happened to the stuffed bear in this story?"
O	Open-ended	These prompts build the students' expressive language by encouraging them to explain action in illustrations.	"Tell me what's happening in this picture."
W	Wh_____	These prompts usually begin with what, where, when, why, and how questions, and help students learn new vocabulary.	While pointing to an object in the book, "What's the name of this?"
D	Distancing	The teacher asks students to relate the pictures or text to something they experienced.	While reading a book about jack o' lanterns say, "Remember when we went to the pumpkin patch? What parts of the pumpkin did we see there that are shown in this picture?"

Source: Whitehurst et al., 1994

With a text this short, you might read it through in its entirety first, pausing to explain unfamiliar ideas or vocabulary. On the second (or even third!) reading, incorporate some of the dialogic reading prompts, such as the following.

- **Completion:** Ask the student to fill in the rhyme, "Jack and Jill went up the _____"

- **Recall:** Ask, "What happened when Jack and Jill went up the hill?"

- **Open-ended:** In an illustrated text copy, point to an illustration and ask, "What's going on in this picture?"

- ***Wh-* prompts:** Ask, "Where are Jack and Jill going?" "What did Jack break?" and "Why are Jack and Jill walking up the hill?"

- **Distancing:** Ask, "Have you ever rolled down a hill?" or "Tell me about a time you fell down. How did it feel?"

Research shows that among low-income students, preschoolers exposed to dialogic reading increased on measures of print awareness, oral language, early writing, and vocabulary (Justice & Ezell, 2004; Justice et al., 2005, 2008; Zucker et al., 2009). A robust body of research documents the benefits of dialogic reading to young learners, which are also easy to enact (What Works Clearinghouse, 2010).

Elementary and Middle School Strategy (grades 3–8): Don't Show the Pictures—at First

In the typical read aloud routine, teachers read a page and then deliberately display the illustrations. Students crane their necks to get a look at the pictures; inevitably a student calls out, "I didn't see the pictures!" In some read alouds—particularly those conducted in elementary classrooms—I recommend teachers *not* show the pictures (at first!). Rest assured, students will get a glimpse of them, but first let me explain my intentionality here.

The aim is to encourage visualization as a comprehension strategy. I use this particular strategy with students in the grades 3–8 range because of the explosion in their development in the visual processing portions of the brain. Milestone research from educational psychologist G. Michael Pressley (1976) indicates visualization improves not only comprehension but also readers' retention and memory of a text. Shanahan (2021) points out that *visualization*—or forming sensory representation—"doesn't help comprehension, it is part of the comprehension process." Shanahan (2021) uncovers research about brain activation during visualization:

> With older proficient readers (8–11 yrs.), they [undergo] activation in the occipital regions of the brain suggesting visual or imaginative processing in the right hemisphere. But this kind of activity is not evident with 5–7-year-olds when they are reading. Instead, their brains appear to be more focused on coordinating the visual representations of the words with phonological processing . . . That means that visualization is evident in reading in grades 3–5, but not so much in grades 1 and 2, at least when it came to reading.

With this strategy, teachers can facilitate students making *mental models*—or visualizing—the text. According to the International Literacy Association's (n.d.) literacy glossary, *visualization* is "the process, or result, of mentally picturing objects or events that are normally experienced directly. Visualizing can be an effective reading strategy for increasing reading comprehension."

Visualization integrates many skills of comprehension; to make a mental image of a text, students must weave together text evidence, their background knowledge, and a dash of creativity to match their imagery with that of the text. Furthermore, visualization encourages students to actively engage with the text, notice the author's choice of descriptive language, synthesize imagery based on incoming information, and connect deeply with the text.

To introduce visualization, model a think aloud from a small portion of particularly descriptive text. Use first-person *I language*, intentionally pointing out that visualization relies on text clues.

Here's an example of a short, descriptive passage from *Charlotte's Web* (White, 1952). You might start your think aloud with this reminder: "I'm going to read this passage aloud and then talk through the images that appear in my mind like a movie. The movie in my mind comes from all the descriptive language the author uses." Here is the passage:

> The barn was very large. It was very old. It smelled of hay and it smelled of manure. It smelled of the perspiration of tired horses and the wonderful sweet breath of patient

cows. It often had a sort of peaceful smell—as though nothing bad could happen ever again in the world. It smelled of grain and of harness dressing and of axle grease and of rubber boots and of new rope. And whenever the cat was given a fish-head to eat, the barn would smell of fish. But mostly it smelled of hay, for there was always hay in the great loft up overhead. And there was always hay being pitched down to the cows and the horses and the sheep. (White, 1952, p. 34)

Here's the think aloud teachers might provide to accompany the passage they read, homing in on the text details that shape their mental imagery:

"In my mind's eye, I see a large wooden barn. It's sitting in a meadow of grass. I think it's in a field because the text tells me that the barn is used for cows, horses, and sheep—so I think those animals would need a pasture to graze in. I'm picturing this barn is at least three stories tall, and it's missing some wood planks. The phrase "very old" makes me think that some of the boards are falling off. I used the clue "the great loft overhead" to paint the picture of this barn being tall and having many stories. In this barn, I'm seeing old farm tools and bales of hay and rusty farm machines. I know that animals—like horses—sometimes sleep in stalls, so I'm seeing separate wooden compartments with beds of hay for animals to sleep on. I used the words rusty and rope to see the tools that a farmer might store in this barn. And the author's given me lots of clues, so I see these bales of hay stacked up and used as bedding for the animals."

With this explanation, readers see the types of details to expand on using visualization.

My Top Five Read Aloud Texts for Visualization and Mental Images

The following list features my favorite titles to encourage visualization for readers of all ages.

de la Peña, M. (2021). *Milo imagines the world* (C. Robinson, Illus.). New York: G.P. Putnam's Sons Books for Young Readers

Frazee, M. (2003). *Roller coaster*. San Diego, CA: Harcourt.

Rhee, H. K. (2020). *The paper kingdom* (P. Campion, Illus.). New York: Random House.

Van Dusen, C. (2009). *The circus ship*. Somerville, MA: Candlewick Press.

Wang, A. (2021). *Watercress* (J. Chin, Illus.). New York: Porter Books.

Visualization is easy to incorporate into your read alouds with a few simple steps and prompts. After selecting a text with particularly descriptive language (that evokes mental images), such as the preceding descriptive passage from *Charlotte's Web* (White, 1952), explain the following to students before reading:

> "This read aloud is going to be a bit different. I'm going to read to you, and as I read, I want you to imagine what is happening. I want you to use the words in the book to make a movie or a picture in your mind. I promise I will show you the pictures, but first I want to hear about what the pictures in your head look like."

During reading, encourage students to sketch their images or describe them to a partner. Ask these questions to help students elicit their visualizations.

- "Describe the picture in your head. What does the movie look like?"
- "What pictures are you seeing?"
- "What words from the text helped you to create that illustration?"
- "What clues did the text give that painted the image in your mind?"
- "How are your mental images the same and different from the ones in the book (after you see the illustrations)?"
- "How do your illustrations help you better understand the story?"

Other students might benefit from these sentence starters, to jump-start their visualizations.

- In my mind's eye, I am seeing . . .
- The details I notice . . .
- The clues I heard from the text to make my picture are . . .
- Here's how I'd describe the picture in my head . . .
- When I hear _____, I see _____ in my head.

After reading, teachers might do a class compare and contrast—either in simple conversation or with a Venn diagram—of students' images versus the ones in the text. The point here is not for students to think their images are "wrong" and those in the text are "right," but rather to notice and observe how the images expand their comprehension, provide additional information, and enhance the text.

Not every text, nor every page, is opportune for this strategy. Try the strategy yourself before turning the task over to students. If visualization aligns easily to the text you select—because of its rich descriptive language—by all means, give it a go. If you struggle to make mental images with a particular text, your students likely will as well. Also note that you can scaffold visualization by starting at the sentence level and gradually increasing the amount of text to longer portions. For those students who might benefit from focusing on text-based clues or could better connect to text through visualization, this strategy—when paired with a richly descriptive text—is a must-try for upper-elementary and middle grades readers.

Early Childhood, Elementary, and Middle School Strategy (grades PreK–8): Jump-Start Student-Generated Questions

Children are naturally curious and come to class well versed in posing questions to their parents and caregivers. On a typical day, children ages two to ten years old typically ask their parents an average of 288 questions (Frazier, Gelman, & Wellman, 2009). According to coauthors Michelle M. Chouinard, P. L. Harris, and Michael P. Maratsos (2007), children ask between four and twelve hundred questions each week. Yet, as children begin formal schooling, their questions often taper off because the instruction provides little room for student-generated questions (Graesser & Person, 1994). Furthermore, the questions students do ask are mostly factual (Chin & Osborne, 2008). In modern classrooms, students answer far more questions than ask questions; the typical student answers an "interminable number of low-level, literal questions" (Allington, 2014, p. 18) with teachers posing three to four hundred questions each day (Levin, 1981).

But what if teachers were to encourage, model, and elicit question generation as a strategy for students to use across any type of text, any content area, and any grade level (Ness, 2016)? Key studies point out proficient readers ask questions, and asking questions is a favorable strategy to enhance reading comprehension (Therrien & Hughes, 2008). Educational consultants and coauthors Stephanie Harvey and Anne Goudvis (2007) explain that questioning pushes readers forward in their understanding of text. In their meta-analysis of question generation, researchers and professors William J. Therrien and Charles Hughes (2008) reported thirteen studies highlighting significant gains in reading comprehension scores with the use of question generation. Professors Ana Taboada and John T. Guthrie (2006) note that question generation contributes to the active reading-comprehension process by helping students initiate cognitive processes, concluding, "When asking questions, students are involved in multiple processes requiring deeper interactions with text" (p. 4). As they pose questions, students become focused readers with stronger understanding of the written text (Chin, Brown, & Bruce, 2002). Question generation also benefits students in other cognitive and motivational capacities. Posing questions builds students' critical-thinking skills and activates higher-level-thinking skills. Students learn to not accept information at face value, but instead to extend their learning in a self-directed manner. More recent research from various disciplines shows question generation improves students' retention of mathematics content (Di Teodoro, Donders, Kemp-Davidson, Robertson, & Schuyler, 2011), explanations of their thinking processes (Gillies, Nichols, Burgh, & Haynes, 2014), engagement in science (Hung , Hwang, Lee, Wu, Vogel, Milrad et al., 2014), and oral and written responses to literature (Peterson & Taylor, 2012). In 2014, a research team from the University of California, Davis, monitored brain activity to measure how engaged learners were in reading questions and their answers (as cited in Singh, 2014). When questions and their answers piqued learners' curiosity, the parts of the brain associated with pleasure, reward, and creation of memory underwent an increase in activity (Singh, 2014). When teachers model how to generate questions, students' question-generation abilities improve (Legare, Mills, Souza, Plummer, & Yasskin, 2013). Sometimes, students need language scaffolds or sentence starters—such as those in the following list—to jump-start their question generation.

- I'm trying to figure out . . .
- I wonder why . . .
- I want to ask . . .
- Here's a question I'm thinking about . . .

As I indicate in the preceding literature, young learners are naturally curious and often do not need explicit instruction in question generation. Rather, students need to understand the value and purpose of their questions. The following two ideas are among my favorite ways to carve out instructional time for question generation during read alouds.

Read Aloud From Simple Text to Generate Complex Questions

For your next read aloud, select a nursery rhyme to model, so sophisticated questions can emerge from a simple text. When I worked with a kindergarten classroom, I used "Jack and Jill" to generate questions collaboratively as table 3.2 outlines.

Table 3.2: Questions Students Generated From a Nursery Rhyme

Nursery Rhyme and Text	Questions Students Posed
Jack and Jill went up the hill To fetch a pail of water. Jack fell down And broke his crown And Jill came tumbling after.	• Why did they have to get water from the top of the hill? Didn't they have water in their house? • Did Jack push Jill? • Why was Jack wearing a crown? • Were they hurt? Did the water spill? • What is the relationship between Jack and Jill? Are they friends? Brother and sister? • Who sent them to get the water? • Where were their parents?

Select a simple, straightforward text (for example, a Shel Silverstein or Jack Prelutsky poem or a nursery rhyme) and model the questions you generate. Students can watch as you think aloud about generating these questions and as you jot them down on sticky notes. Using the *gradual release of responsibility* technique (Pearson & Gallagher, 1983), select a text with a similar format (for example, if you use one nursery rhyme to model, try another nursery rhyme next) to invite students to engage in guided practice. When you're confident students are ready for independent practice, have them try it solo, in pairs, or in small groups. Encourage students to jot their question on one side of the sticky note and on the reverse side, their initials and the text associated with their question. That way, when it's time to showcase powerful questions—and how to address them—you can credit the questioner and engage that student in a conversation about the origin of the question.

Place Read Aloud–Related Questions in a Classroom Parking Lot

Any teacher (and parent!) knows kids ask the darndest things, and sometimes teachers and parents simply don't have answers to their questions. To honor the questions students pose and show them the power of question generation, embrace *parking lots* in the classroom to house those unanswerable questions. The *parking lot* is simply a dedicated classroom space where unanswered questions—jotted down on sticky notes—are placed so the class might visit them when time allows, research their answers in weekly trips to the library, or use them as a launchpad for independent inquiry projects (Ness, 2014).

Take, for instance, my eight-year-old niece, who posed a question as we stargazed one night. I pointed out the Big Dipper and Little Dipper. With a quizzical look, she asked me, "What happened to the Medium Dipper?" On the surface, this question is unanswerable, but what a thoughtful question and a great one to explore! On returning home, we jotted down her question on a sticky note, and then later visited our public library for a child-friendly book that explains the origin of constellations. And as so often happens with children, questions beget questions. The more she learned, the more she asked—leading to an authentic cycle of self-directed learning and looking to text to address her questions.

Though this example occurred outside school walls, parking lots are easily applicable to read alouds. With little more than an allotted section of a door or bulletin board and a handful of sticky notes, your class and you can create an intentional way to encourage question generation to further comprehension, increase engagement and motivation, and purposefully search for text to address students' wonderings (Ness, 2019b).

Model, model, model! Further, since this strategy requires little advance preparation, just have the willingness to seize the next opportunity when a seemingly off-topic or unanswerable question arises. With a classroom parking lot, teachers can enthusiastically embrace the question and model writing it and placing it in the designated spot. Be sure your parking lot isn't a place where questions go to die! The next trip to the school library or any bonus, unplanned minutes are the opportune times to model using text to find the answers to those important pressing questions.

Elementary and Middle School Strategy (grades 3–8): Read From Diverse Text Diets

Chances are, you are familiar with a graphic that depicts what portion of your diet should consist of what food group (see the MyPlate Graphics at https://myplate.gov/resources/graphics/myplate-graphics). Health care providers use this depiction as a reminder that a balance of foods—an ideal mix of proteins, vegetables, starches, and more—is best. As teachers read aloud, they must embrace a similar balance of texts of various genres and complexities. In a 2017 article, reading researcher Elfrieda H. Hiebert outlines the notion of *text diets*, which she defines as, "the accumulation of texts that students read in schools" (p. 125). A subsequent article notes that text diets should ensure "students receive both accessible and challenging texts . . . over a school year and across the school years" (Smith & Hiebert, 2022).

This principle should apply to the texts teachers select for read alouds; just as people balance their healthy fats with produce for a well-rounded diet, teachers should read aloud from diverse and robust text diets. This entails using books of various formats, lengths, genres, complexities, and difficulties. One approach is to approach text diets topically or thematically; once you determine the topic or content for the read aloud, incorporate related materials. Although instructional time might not allow for read alouds of every text included in that text diet, try to read aloud from a short portion of each of them. At the very least, you now have a robust text set that invites students to follow up your central read aloud with related materials.

Now, I'll walk through the creation of a text diet for a fourth-grade classroom about to explore female social justice leaders. Specifically, the focus is on Shirley Chisholm, the first Black woman elected to the U.S. Congress. Knowing you want texts of varying difficulty, aim for texts at three levels: low, medium, and high difficulty (but be careful not to let students know the different levels).

1. *Low-difficulty texts* are accessible to readers below grade level, with less sophisticated vocabulary, shorter format, and more general approachability.

2. *Medium-difficulty texts* are at the corresponding grade level and accessible at students' instructional reading levels.

3. *High-difficulty texts* are more sophisticated in vocabulary, length, and difficulty.

Your main consideration is the accessibility of the text, but be mindful to include a variety of formats, genres, and lengths, as table 3.3 shows.

Table 3.3: A Fourth-Grade Text Diet Focusing on Shirley Chisholm

Low Difficulty		Medium Difficulty		High Difficulty	
Text	Format	Text	Format	Text	Format
Not Done Yet: Shirley Chisholm's Fight for Change (Brown, 2022)	Historical fiction picture book	*Shirley Chisholm Dared: The Story of the First Black Woman in Congress* (Williams, 2021)	Historical fiction picture book	Shirley Chisholm's 1970 Equal Rights Amendment Speech	Speech
Shirley Chisholm (Calkhoven, 2021)	Early chapter book	*Shirley Chisholm Is a Verb* (Chambers, 2020)	Historical fiction picture book	*Shirley Chisholm: The Last Interview and Other Conversations* (Chisholm, 2020)	Autobiography, interviews
It's Her Story Shirley Chisholm (Aggs, 2021)	Graphic novel			*Speak Up, Speak Out! The Extraordinary Life of Fighting Shirley Chisholm* (Bolden, 2022)	Biography
She Was the First! The Trailblazing Life of Shirley Chisholm (Russell-Brown, 2020)	Historical fiction picture book				

As you create your own text diets centering on a central text, use these guidelines and considerations to guide your planning.

- Select a central theme or topic. From there, home in on your primary read aloud.

- With your central read aloud in mind, build out your medium-difficulty category. Include additional resources to add new information, present different opinions, focus on different ideas, or enhance the content. From that group of texts, earmark portions of each text to read aloud, and engage students in making connections and disconnections from these additional resources to your central read aloud.

- Think about your readers not yet on grade level. What types of support would build their understanding of your central text? Think through the types of texts your students find appealing, approachable, and select independently, including graphic novels, novels in verse, shorter texts, and easier picture books. As you select portions of simpler text to read aloud, be sure to focus on how these versions reflect, confirm, or clarify the ideas from the central text.

- Select texts more complex in layout, vocabulary, and sentence structure to include in your high-difficulty portion. Select shorter portions of these texts to read aloud, ensuring you think aloud through any potential points of confusion. Engage students in conversations where they synthesize their overarching understanding with new understanding of the more sophisticated text shapes.

- There does not need to be an equal number of texts at each level, but the levels should reflect the approximate breakdown of your students. In other words, if you've got a larger number of students reading below grade level, include more low-difficulty selections.

- Don't let students know where each text falls in complexity; each text provides a valuable contribution. Teachers must consciously fight against the notion that texts are "good" or "bad" based on the level of complexity or difficulty.

- Be creative in your inclusion of texts of varying difficulty and accessibility. Magazine articles, how-to books, interviews, poems, and memoirs all enhance the richness of a text diet.

A Call to Action

This chapter opened with the data revealing the frequency of read alouds decline as students age (Scholastic, n.d.). Once teachers are consciously aware of that trend, they have the ability to fight against it—intentionally reading aloud in classrooms for students of all grades—particularly those serving upper-elementary and middle school students. Practical ideas like dialogic reading and print-focused read alouds help younger students build oral language and print conventions, while question generation, visualizing, and text diets are particularly fruitful for older readers.

As you recommit to reading aloud using this chapter's five strategies, reflect on these questions.

- What are your current practices to encourage visualization as a comprehension strategy? As you tried this strategy, what were your students' reactions? How was this read aloud experience different for them and for you?

- If you teach in early childhood classrooms (PreK and kindergarten, for instance), how might you incorporate print-focused read alouds into your instructional routines? How did your students react? Make note of any evidence where you noticed an impact on students' early literacy skills and attention to printed text.

- How do you typically address student-generated questions? In what ways do you encourage students to ask questions, and how do you honor those they've posed? How do you connect your read alouds to question generation?

- After keeping a log of student-generated questions over a few days of instruction, what do you notice? How do you address these questions? What are some of the best questions students posed?

- If you teach in an early childhood classroom, reflect on dialogic reading. How much of your read alouds use teacher-dominated language? In what ways do your read alouds facilitate, enhance, and elicit students' oral language?

- How might you carve out more opportunities for language exchanges with students as you read aloud?

- What do you notice about your students' text diets? What are their diets rich in? Where are deficiencies in their diets? How might you use read alouds to diversify their text diets?

- Create a text diet about an area of focus—a particular topic or area you will soon cover in instruction (as in the example for Shirley Chisholm, page 70). What did you discover in the experience?

CHAPTER 4

Customize Read Alouds for Various Content Areas

Up to this point, I've examined read alouds that occur largely in the language arts classroom or reading block. However, part of this book's purpose is that there can—and should—be a time, place, value, and rationale for read alouds across *all* content-area classrooms through middle school. To tackle the challenge of reading aloud in all subject areas, I offer unpacking guidelines. Whereas previous chapters examined read alouds in the context of the planning template, here I present a modified version of that approach for read alouds across the content areas. This planning process is a bit more expedited and laser focused on supporting students before, during, and after the read aloud.

This chapter opens with research-supported information about the need for read alouds across content areas. Next, it moves into instructions on planning a content-area read aloud. You will also find individual sections on reading aloud in social studies, science, mathematics, music, physical education, and the arts. Within the sections, I offer tips for how to do read alouds in different subjects (for example, music) in which it might be hard to conceptualize reading aloud in an engaging way that extends learning. I also include a wealth of examples, lists of books, and other resources to share with your students. The chapter closes with the repeating A Call to Action section, with questions to use to reflect on chapter content. To begin, I'll examine the rationale for reading aloud in a variety of subjects outside the language arts.

Understanding the Need for Read Alouds Across Content Areas

In the American public education system, students spend a minimum of 180 days in school, with an average school day five to six hours long. Though there may be uniformity in the scope of the academic calendar, the allotment of instructional time differs significantly across districts and states—and even across grade levels. In her best-selling book, *The Knowledge Gap*, Wexler (2019) explains that the bulk of the instructional day in elementary schools is spent either in the mathematics or the English language arts block. Consequently, instructional time in other content areas has plummeted. Data from a national survey of teachers and principals support this claim, showing the following allocation of instructional minutes in third grade in public schools (Taie & Goldring, 2020).

- A weekly average of 540 minutes of instruction per week in English, reading, and language arts
- 370 minutes in arithmetic or mathematics
- 170 minutes in science
- 60 minutes in social studies or history

Wexler (2019) argues that the United States' declining test scores in reading are a consequence of students' lack of background knowledge in various content areas. The more students know about mathematics, science, and social studies, the more this background knowledge improves their ability to make meaning of any texts they encounter. An important way to build background knowledge across these content areas is, therefore, to read aloud across grade levels and content areas.

There's both good news and bad news: 23 percent of middle school teachers report reading aloud to students every day, but 27 percent report never reading aloud (Scholastic, n.d.). These findings, however, may be a bit misleading because teacher-led read alouds occur most frequently from content-area textbooks. Teachers often espouse that students cannot read the textbook, so they often accommodate them by reading it aloud while students follow along silently. In this chapter, I focus on read alouds in content areas from texts *other than* traditional textbooks. These read alouds—and their associated activities—support students' literacy skills in content-area instruction, as well as comprehension and retention of presented material.

Give specific attention to multiple series of books, which have multiple cross-content-area applications. As these titles and offerings expand, nearly every content-area teacher will be able to find a title for an appropriate classroom read aloud. Keep in mind: a read aloud does not need to cover the text in its entirety; content-area read alouds you can complete in five to ten minutes can be effective. For this reason, consider incorporating many anthologies, as in the following list.

- The *Who Was?* series is highly popular and has nearly three hundred titles about stories of past and present innovators and trailblazers. An art teacher might read aloud from *Who Was Georgia O'Keeffe?* (Fabiny, 2022), whereas a gym teacher might select *Who Are Venus and Serena Williams?* (Buckley, 2017). The series now includes *Where Is?* and *What Was?* titles.
- Brad Meltzer's (2014–2023) *Ordinary People Change the World* series is appropriate for elementary students, and the variety of these books is impressive, covering historical figures from Walt Disney and Lucille Ball to Jane Goodall.

- The *She Persisted* series (Clinton, 2017) focuses on women's empowerment. This series of picture books and chapter books tell the stories of women who stood up, spoke up, and rose up against the odds! A social studies teacher might read aloud from *Harriet Tubman* (Pinkney, 2021), whereas a physical education teacher might select the story of prima ballerina *Maria Tallchief* (Day, 2021).

- The *Little People, BIG DREAMS* series (Vergara, 2016–2023) is a best-selling series of books that explores the lives of outstanding people from designers and artists to scientists and activists. Presenting ideal read alouds for grades PreK–2 classrooms, the series covers iconic historians, artists, leaders, and others.

- Vashti Harrison's (2017–2019) *Little Leaders* series shines the light on bold Black men and women across the globe; these minibiographies make perfect short read alouds for any content area.

- The *Good Night Stories for Rebel Girls* (Favilli & Cavallo, 2016–2022) book series has endless possibilities and now includes an app with stories of fearless, adventurous women in sports, science, and history. Teachers can find short biographies of women whose contributions are relevant to any content area. The release of *Stories for Boys Who Dare to Be Different* (Brooks, 2018) has a similar format, purposefully highlighting men who don't adhere to the stereotypical idea of masculinity. The beauty of these books is that each biography is one page, leading to quick, easy read alouds you can complete in five minutes or less.

- Author Catherine Thimmesh (2018, 2022) and illustrator Melissa Sweet have put out visually gorgeous and affirming volumes perfect for science and social studies: *Girls Think of Everything: Stories of Ingenious Inventions by Women* and *Girls Solve Everything: Stories of Women Entrepreneurs Building a Better World*.

- Rockridge Press created a series of books perfect to highlight the contributions of Black scientists, historians, and leaders: *Black Leaders in the Civil Rights Movement: A Black history book for kids* (Armand, 2021); *Black Men in Science: A Black History Book for Kids* (Avery, 2022); *Black Inventors: 15 Inventions That Changed the World* (Trusty, 2021); and *Black Women in Science: A Black History Book for Kids* (Pellum, 2019).

- Rockridge Press also offers Jimmy Beason's (2021) *Native Americans in History: A History Book for Kids* and Tina Cho's (2022) *Asian American Women in Science: An Asian American History Book for Kids*.

- Read aloud from Kelly Yang's (2022) gorgeous picture book *Yes We Will: Asian Americans Who Shaped This Country*. Or explore how Muslim leaders have contributed to society in *The Wonders We Seek: 30 Incredible Muslims Who Helped Shape the World* (Faruqi & Mumtaz, 2022). Similarly, I'm fond of *Courageous History Makers: 11 Women From Latin America Who Changed the World* (Reynoso, 2021).

- Also for elementary readers, Rockridge Press offers an entire series (*The Story Of: A Biography Series for New Readers*; Katz et al., 2020–2023). These short, engaging biographies offer the perfect read aloud for teachers of all levels and content areas.

• Keeping in mind that texts should feature people of differing ability levels, enjoy the 2020 compilation titled *I Am Not a Label: 34 Disabled Artists, Thinkers, Athletes and Activists From Past and Present* (Burnell, 2020).

Planning the Content-Area Read Aloud

Much of the planning for a content-area read aloud mirrors the previous planning process (see chapter 1, page 17). You'll recognize the evaluate, explain, and engage-and -extend format, but there are a few ways teachers should tweak read alouds for content areas. The first planning step is largely the same: evaluate a text for areas to activate and build background knowledge. During the reading, clarify and explain the text. Because read alouds in content areas are often meant to foster students' understanding of specific content or a specific topic, the bulk of your instruction should focus on supporting read- ers before, during, and after reading to maximize their understanding and retention of the material. Subdivide the explain step into what you will explain before, during, and after reading. To extend support through think alouds, clarify unfamiliar vocabulary or points of confusion. After reading, support students' retention and comprehension of newly acquired information through higher-order-thinking questions and other litera- cy-based activities. For the third step, engage and extend, further explore the topic and brainstorm instructional opportunities to build meaning through literacy. You can also extend learning opportunities to learners with diverse needs and reading levels, keeping in mind the need for differentiation. See the planning template for content-area read alouds in figure 4.1.

Evaluate	To understand this text, readers need the following background knowledge.		
Explain	Before	During	After
Engage and Extend			

Figure 4.1: Planning template for content-area read alouds.

Visit go.SolutionTree.com/literacy to download this page

The following sections offer examples of content-area texts for read alouds to apply to this template so it is easy to see how this tool works across content areas.

Reading Aloud in Social Studies

According to the National Council for the Social Studies (2010), social studies is a rich interdisciplinary field integrating history, economics, geography, civics, sociology, anthropology, archaeology, and psychology. For too long, American schools deprioritized social studies; in a 2014 survey, early elementary teachers reported an average of sixteen instructional minutes a day in social studies (Fitchett, Heafner, & VanFossen, 2014). Subsequently, student performance in high-stakes social studies testing is subpar. Among eighth graders, only 18 percent scored proficient or above in U.S. history, with similar results in civics (23 percent) and geography (27 percent; Fitchett et al., 2014).

To complicate matters, much of social studies instruction comes from textbooks. Reading from a textbook peaks as a classroom activity in the intermediate elementary grades and high school grades. At the secondary level, reading aloud occurs more often in social studies than in any other core subject (Wakefield, 2006). These textbooks are often problematic, as thought leaders point out: social studies textbooks are often above students' reading levels (Sheridan-Thomas, 2014) and have long ignored the contributions of Black, Indigenous, and other people of color (Gewertz, 2020).

Considering that the lack of prioritizing frequent, meaningful social studies instruction, as well as the problematic reliance on textbooks, social studies classes provide prime opportunities to incorporate read alouds. Social studies read alouds take many forms outside the traditional textbook—from primary documents like journal entries and diaries to magazine and newspaper clippings and informational texts focusing on one specific time period or historical figure.

Pretend you're inside a middle school social studies classroom for a moment, like the one I used to teach. I love incorporating read alouds into monthly celebrations, so here I focus on March as the chance to celebrate Women's History Month. I select the historical fiction picture book *Amelia and Eleanor Go for a Ride* by Pam Muñoz Ryan (1999). With its striking black and white etchings from artist Brian Selznick, this book features two notable women—First Lady and social justice pioneer Eleanor Roosevelt and pilot Amelia Earhart—and their little-known friendship. To highlight the notion you can determine much about people by their words, I select a reading activity modified from Hallie Kay Yopp and Ruth Helen Yopp's (2014) characters' quotes.

Prior to the read aloud, select a handful of quotes from both central characters (culled from their speeches, interviews, and writings). I purposefully select quotes that hint at the historical figures' beliefs, identities, and contributions. Importantly, these quotes are *not* taken from the book but rather, directly from the two historical figures (written or spoken). Write those quotes (see figure 4.2, page 78) on two different colored index cards. Intentionally do not tell students who the quotes are from or the title of the text; you want them to use the quotes to make predictions and inferences without the influence of their background knowledge. Display a T-chart with two columns: *What I Notice* and *What I Wonder*. Give each student an index card, and then model how you use the quote to wonder and predict about the kind of person who might write or say the words on the card. You might borrow from this explanation:

> Each of you has a card with words that come from two different famous historical women. The yellow cards come from one woman, and the purple cards come from the other. I'm not going to tell you who said these words or when they lived, but your job is to act like historians and figure out what you might infer about these people, what was important to them, and why they are part of our celebration for Women's History Month. Remember, you can learn a lot

about someone in history by the words they spoke or wrote, and that's why you've got some words as clues.

I'll show you how to do it with my purple card. It says, "The woman who can create her own job is the woman who will win fame and fortune." I can tell this person might be hardworking since she values her own job. I'm going to jot down hardworking under What I Notice. This quote makes me wonder if this person is a woman, so I'm jotting that question down under What I Wonder.

Give students the chance to try this with their card, and then invite them to find a student who has another card of the same color (and person). In a mock tea party, students mix and mingle with their classmates—some of whom have the same color card and some who have the other color—so they have multiple sources of information to modify and build their predictions about the characters. Not only does this activity ask students to make predictions and inferences about their upcoming reading but it also sets the purpose for the read aloud of the shared text: to determine who spoke the words and the accuracy of the students' initial thoughts about the characters.

Quotes from Eleanor Roosevelt (written on yellow index cards)	• "A woman is like a tea bag—you can't tell how strong she is until you put her in hot water." • "Great minds discuss ideas; average minds discuss events; small minds discuss people." • "Have convictions. Be friendly. Stick to your beliefs as they stick to theirs. Work as hard as they do." • "I believe that anyone can conquer fear by doing the things he fears to do, provided he keeps doing them until he gets a record of successful experience behind him." • "It is not fair to ask of others what you are not willing to do yourself." • "It is not more vacation we need—it is more vocation." • "You have to accept whatever comes and the only important thing is that you meet it with courage and with the best that you have to give."
Quotes from Amelia Earhart (written on purple index cards)	• "Adventure is worthwhile in itself." • "I want to do it because I want to do it." • "Never do things others can do and will do, if there are things others cannot do or will not do." • "The most difficult thing is the decision to act; the rest is merely tenacity. The fears are paper tigers. You can do anything you decide to do. You can act to change and control your life." • "No kind action ever stops with itself. One kind action leads to another. A good example is followed. A single act of kindness throws out roots in all directions, and the roots spring up and make new trees. The greatest work that kindness does to others is that it makes them kind themselves." • "Women, like men, should try to do the impossible. And when they fail, their failure should be but a challenge to others." • "Women must try to do things as men have tried." • "Experiment! Meet new people. That's better than any college education. . . . By adventuring about, you become accustomed to the unexpected. The unexpected then becomes what it really is—the inevitable."

Source: BrainyQuote, n.d.a, n.d.b; Goodreads, n.d.

Figure 4.2: Quotes to use prior to reading aloud from *Amelia and Eleanor Go for a Ride* (Ryan, 1999).

An activity such as this can serve as the basis for planning an entire read aloud in social studies, as you'll see from the way I completed the content-areas planning template (see figure 4.3, page 80).

Even though I explore just one historical fiction text in detail, the following suggestions are largely applicable to whatever social studies content or topic you are teaching, so tailor them to the time period or historical event of relevance to you.

- Read aloud from historical figures' speeches (see https://americanrhetoric.com/speechbank.htm).

- Studying a war? Read aloud from the letters of soldiers during the Civil War, World War I, and so on (see the online database of the National Archives at https://archives.gov/research/databases).

- Read aloud journal entries for your time period (for example, the resources at https://rareamericana.com include those from a woman living through post–Civil War Reconstruction).

- Read aloud from obituaries of leaders and political figures.

- Select a date in history and find a newspaper's front page to read aloud (see https://newspapers.com and https://reutersagency.com/en).

- Choose a selection from *Honest History* magazine (see https://honesthistory.co/collections/magazines) and compare it to how textbook versions explain a particular person or event.

As you read aloud in social studies—from primary sources like speeches, newspaper clippings about current events, and biographies of political leaders—you show students that social studies is the connection from past to present, the exploration of the world and its events, and an essential element in an informed citizenry.

	To understand this text, readers need the following background knowledge.
Evaluate	Eleanor Roosevelt: First Lady, activist for women's rights and human rights Amelia Earhart: First solo airplane flight across the Atlantic Ocean Setting and context of 1933, Great Depression White House as a sophisticated, formal setting Women and men not seen as equals; did not earn same salaries, women restricted to the kinds of work they could do Etiquette during fancy dinner parties

	Before	During	After
Explain	• Model and explain corresponding engagement activity. • Give students two minutes to silently read their card, and to think quietly about what their card means. • Display a T-chart for the class with the column headers, What I Notice and What I Wonder. • Direct students to jot down what they notice and wonder about in their readers' notebook. As students work, circulate to students who might need extra support and act as their scribe, if necessary. • After two minutes, have students find a neighbor who has a different color card than theirs. • Have students follow this format: (1) listen to their partners read their card, (2) listen to their partners share what they notice and wonder about, (3) share their card aloud, (4) share their What I Notice and What I Wonder with their partner, and (5) see if there are any commonalities or similarities in the two cards. • Lead students in sharing what they notice and wonder about. You might use different colored pens to denote the two different colored cards, or you might record students' responses under two different T-charts. • If students have not guessed the identity of these historical figures, tell them. • Display photos of both women.	• Explain the words outspoken and determined. See if any of the initial student wonderings align with those words. • Pages 4-5: Do a think aloud with the full-page spread of the White House, modeling inferences with "I'm getting the sense it's spring as there are flowers on these trees." • Pages 6-9: Model thinking aloud about the similarities between the women-such as wearing gloves and their approach to independence. "I'm noticing these women have a lot in common-from the way they dress to how they are daring and independent." • Pages 14-15: Ask students to deduce how the guests at the dinner table are feeling based on the illustrations. • Pages 18-21: Connect the women's actions to some of the initial student noticings from T-chart. (For example, say, "Originally we said the character might be fearless, and I'm getting the sense this is true.") • Pages 24-27: Think aloud: "It's important for me to remember this book takes place during a time when people thought women could not do as many things as men, so it would be very shocking to see women fly a plane and drive a car at night-especially if one of them is the First Lady!"	• Revisit the initial noticings students generate from the character quotes. Discuss the ways in which the book supports and refutes students' original noticings. • Revisit the original wonderings to see if the author addressed any in the book. Encourage students to generate new wonderings based on the book. You might model with statements like, "I wonder if Eleanor ever got her pilot license." • Pose higher-order questions, like the following: + "What lessons can people learn from these women who did not follow gender expectations?" + "Why is the time frame of this book an important consideration?" + "Choose one of the quotes, either from Amelia or Eleanor. Explain how this story relates to that quote."

Engage and Extend	Create a Venn diagram comparing and contrasting Amelia and Eleanor. Have students pretend they are Eleanor Roosevelt. Have them write entries in their diaries describing their night with Amelia Earhart. Search for videos of author interviews online and watch an interview with author Pam Muñoz Ryan. Ask students, "How does watching this deepen your understanding of the story?" Have students revisit their initial thoughts from the character quotes and discuss how the characters' actions connected or didn't connect with the characters' actions in the story.

Figure 4.3: Completed content-area read aloud planning template for *Amelia and Eleanor Go for a Ride* (Ryan, 1999).

Reading Aloud in Science

When I was a student, my understanding of what science entailed was simplistic and narrow. I also had a limited understanding of scientists; in my mind, all scientists looked like Einstein. They were White men in lab coats standing over bubbling test tubes on Bunsen burners. Fortunately, more expansive and inclusive depictions of scientists are available for today's students. Picture books like *Ada Twist, Scientist* (Beaty, 2016) and television shows like *Sid the Science Kid* (Zweig, 2008) and *Doc McStuffins* (Fontana, 2012) demonstrate how science is everywhere and available for all to partake in. Additionally, modern science standards have far more breadth and include four interdisciplinary areas: (1) life sciences, (2) earth and space sciences, (3) physical sciences, and (4) engineering, technology, and application of science (Next Generation Science Standards [NGSS] Lead States, 2013).

Teachers are increasingly incorporating trade books into science instruction (Broemmel, Rearden, & Buckner, 2021), not only for their approachable explanation to background knowledge (Cervetti, Barber, Dorph, Pearson, & Goldschmidt, 2012) but also their exposure to diverse scientists (Lovedahl & Bricker, 2006). University of Central Florida education professors Rebeca A. Grysko and Vassiliki I. Zygouris-Coe (2020) highlight how reading aloud and discussing scientific texts support students' knowledge building, vocabulary, and understanding of science textbook structures. I'm particularly fond of using picture books to simplify the abstract and esoteric ideas of science. My mind was blown in discovering a picture book about *nanoscience* (the discovery and creation of materials). Undoubtedly, my tenth-grade self would have benefited from a read aloud of author Jess Wade's (2021) *Nano: The Spectacular Science of the Very (Very) Small* in chemistry. See figure 4.4, (page 82) for an example of how to use the content-area planning template to support a science read aloud for this text.

Following are additional books for science read alouds, with a particular focus on diversity in the field.

For women's contributions in science, read aloud from these titles.

- *Wonder Women of Science: 12 Geniuses Who Are Currently Rocking Science, Technology, and the World* (Fletcher & Rue, 2021)
- *Grace Hopper: Queen of Computer Code* (Wallmark, 2017)

For scientists from diverse backgrounds, ethnicities, abilities, and sexual orientations, read aloud from these titles.

- *Queen of Physics: How Wu Chien Shiung Helped Unlock the Secrets of the Atom* (Robeson, 2019)
- *The World Is Not a Rectangle: A Portrait of Architect Zaha Hadid* (Winter, 2017)
- *STEM* (Dufresne, (2021b)
- *The Girl Who Thought in Pictures: The Story of Dr. Temple Grandin* (Mosca, 2017)

Need other engaging science topics for read alouds? Weather makes for a highly appealing read aloud topic, as it's relevant every day. How about reading aloud from newspaper clippings about weather patterns and then exploring those phenomena through the National Geographic weather series (see https://nationalgeographic.org/education/extreme-weather)? Or explore the daily online Farmer's Almanac to understand how weather patterns and

	Before	During	After
Evaluate	To understand this text, readers need the following background knowledge. • A basic understanding that materials are composed of atoms • That atoms are invisible to the human eye, but visible with powerful microscopes • A general understanding of the role and use of microscopes • That scientists are constantly testing, inventing, encountering failures, observing mistakes, and using these mistakes to adapt		
Explain	• Remind students that chemistry is the study of matter and how matter changes. • Define molecules as atoms bonded together. • Have students build basic diagrams of molecules using toothpicks as bonds and marshmallows or gumdrops as molecules. • Display the periodic table to remind students that elements are made of a single type of atom.	• Display the cover and explain that nano means tiny. Encourage students to share out terms they've heard with nano, like nanosecond. • Pages 2-3: Have students point out or name the materials they see in the classroom. • Page 4: Pose these questions: "What do you think makes different materials light or strong? Heavy or flexible? Why is a rock heavy but glass is delicate?" Have students generate predictions in turn and talks. • Page 5: Ask students, "What does a microscope show? How does a microscope help you understand what materials are made of?" • Pages 6-7: Have students turn to a partner to define atoms. Have students turn to a partner and define molecules. Model a think aloud to synthesize by saying, "The big idea here is that atoms make up everything around you, and atoms form molecules." • Pages 8-9: Have students call out elements they remember or have encountered. Point out these elements in a displayed periodic table. • Pages 10-11: Ask students to share out examples of carbon they've heard. • Pages 12-13: Have students recount the advantages of graphene. • Pages 14-15: Have students make some predictions on how people use graphene in their everyday lives. Check these predictions against the examples provided on pages 16-19. • Pages 20-21: Clarify what sieves are, and their multiple uses. • Pages 22-23: Encourage students to brainstorm additional uses of nanomaterials.	Use a word web graphic organizer, with nanomaterial in the center of the web. Add terms like graphene, carbon, and other terms the text boldfaces as offshoots of the web. Use the web to help students understand the relationship between these terms.
Engage and Extend	• Have students look into nanoscience and nanotechnology on websites you preselect. • Explore the Nanoscience Classroom Resources from the National Science Foundation (see https://nsf.gov/news/classroom/nano.jsp). • Have students listen to the author's interview from Imperial College (see https://youtube.com/watch?v=WYhRUPX2QKY).		

Figure 4.4: Completed content-area read aloud planning template for *Nano* (Wade, 2021).

moon cycles influence gardening (see https://almanac.com). Books about nature and the environment also hook readers. I can't stop thinking about the hidden communication system of trees explored in *The Gentle Genius of Trees* (Bunting, 2023). Animals are always a safe bet to appeal to students. How about Jess Keating's (2016, 2019, 2021) popular series: *Pink Is for Blobfish: Discovering the World's Perfectly Pink Animals*; *Gross as a Snot Otter: Discovering the World's Most Disgusting Animals*; and *Big as a Giant Snail: Discovering the World's Most Gigantic Animals*? I've also yet to meet a student who doesn't express interest in space. Tap into that natural curiosity with these titles: *If You Had Your Birthday Party on the Moon* (Lapin, 2019), *How We Got to the Moon: The People, Technology, and Daring Feats of Science Behind Humanity's Greatest Adventure* (Rocco, 2020), or for younger elementary readers particularly, *Mae Among the Stars* (Ahmed, 2018). And as a parent, I fully agree with this quote from the *New York Times*, "Books about butts, farts, poop, and burps are guaranteed to impress children" (Parker-Pope, 2022). Let your students squeal and giggle over the gross facts in *Kay's Anatomy: A Complete (and Completely Disgusting) Guide to the Human Body* (Kay, 2020).

Reading Aloud in Mathematics

Of all the content areas, mathematics is arguably the most difficult to connect to reading aloud, as "literacy work in math classrooms remains underspecified and underexplored" (Ippolito, Dobbs, & Charner-Laird, 2017, p. 67). However, a growing body of research shows incorporating read alouds into mathematics promotes the following rich benefits (as cited in Hintz & Smith, 2021).

- Improves kindergartners' mathematics performance on numbers, measurement, and geometry (van den Heuvel-Panhuizen, Elia, & Robitzsch, 2016)

- Increases scores in listening comprehension, word problem scores, and number identification (Moussa, Koester, & Alonge, 2018)

- Promotes deeper conceptual knowledge, real-life application, and acquisition of general mathematical literacy (Ippolito et al., 2017)

Researchers Marja van den Heuvel-Panhuizen and Iliada Elia (2012) highlight how students' literacy can build context for mathematics, make connections between mathematics and students' lives, generate interest about mathematics, and promote the use of mathematical processes like problem solving, reasoning, and inquiry. An article from coauthors Terrell A. Young, Eula Ewing Monroe, and Amy Roth-McDuffie (2021) indicates elementary students deepen their conceptual understanding and mathematics vocabulary through read alouds from picture book biographies.

I'll admit it—mathematics was neither my favorite nor my strongest subject in school. (Perhaps I would have benefited from hearing a read aloud of British author Anna Claybourne's [2019] *I Can Be a Math Magician*.) Partly, I disliked mathematics because I didn't see its relevance to my life. Yes, I was that student who mumbled, "When in my life am I ever going to use this?" as I slogged through cosines, derivatives, and logarithms. Now, I watch my own child ask these same questions as she complains about her prealgebra homework, but I have the perspective now to understand—mathematics is fundamental to the structures of current and historical societies. Mathematics has its own language, and to read and think like a mathematician, students must understand the words of that language. Enter the power of reading aloud in mathematics—in particular, using picture books to simplify the abstract concepts.

The other day, I opened up Facebook to the image of a triangle with lines delineating other triangles within it. As a challenge, a friend asked others to give the total sum of triangles in the image. I scrolled through the chain of friends and colleagues trying to outsmart each other and thought back to my ninth-grade mathematics teacher, Mr. Stephens. Surely, he'd take delight in this challenge of *fractals*—the complex patterns that can continue infinitely. In simpler terms, fractals are never-ending patterns. Confused? You're not alone. A 2013 study across middle and high school shows students have misunderstandings and lack knowledge about fractals (Karakus, 2013). Whereas students can often identify fractals, they struggle to find and formulate pattern rules for fractals. Thankfully, a picture book, *Mysterious Patterns: Finding Fractals in Nature* by award-winning author and photo illustrator Sarah C. Campbell (2014) clarifies this concept. With its glossary, straightforward text, and photos, this book simplifies an abstract concept while illuminating the relevance of fractals. Here's how a mathematics teacher—like Mr. Stephens—might read aloud from this picture book to provide background knowledge, elucidate a new concept, and create real-life relevance (see figure 4.5)

Following are additional titles to convince students of the relevance, pervasiveness, and pertinence of mathematics in everyday life.

- *What's the Point of Math?* (Davis & Mubeen, 2020)
- *The Language of the Universe: A Visual Exploration of Mathematics* (Stuart, 2019)
- *It's a Numberful World: How Math Is Hiding Everywhere* (Woo, 2019)
- *Tangled: A Story About Shapes* (Miranda, 2019)
- *The Book of Math: Adventures in the World of Shapes and Numbers* (Weltman, 2021)

There are also ample titles to help remind students of the joy and fun in mathematics, including the *Math Is CATegorical* series (Cleary, 2005–2014) from Millbrook Press, and the beloved picture and riddle books from educator and author Greg Tang (2001), known for *The Grapes of Math*. You might start every mathematics lesson with a short excerpt from any of the thirteen mystery books from the *Charlesbridge Math Adventures* (Neuschwander, Einhorn, Kroll, & Sparagna LoPresti, 1997–2014). Even your most mathematics-resistant readers will be hooked on read alouds featuring the mathematics behind sports in *It's a Numbers Game! Basketball: The Math Behind the Perfect Bounce Pass, the Buzzer-Beating Bank Shot, and So Much More!* (Buckley, 2020) and *The Math of the Games* series (*Baseball*, Adamson, 2011a; *Basketball*, Adamson, 2011b; *Football*, Frederick, 2011a; *Hockey*, Frederick, 2011b). And do not overlook biographies and memoirs of fascinating mathematicians, including the following.

- *Maryam's Magic: The Story of Mathematician Maryam Mirzakhani* (Reid, 2021)
- *Hidden Figures: The True Story of Four Black Women and the Space Race* (Shetterly, 2018)
- *The Girl With a Mind for Math: The Story of Raye Montague* (Mosca, 2018)
- *Emmy Noether: The Most Important Mathematician You've Never Heard Of* (Becker, 2020)

		Before	During	After
Evaluate			To understand this text, readers need the following background knowledge. Understanding of flat shapes versus 3-D shapes Familiarity with a book's glossary The ability to recognize objects in nature (like broccoli, the wildflower Queen Anne's lace, and bolts of lightning)	

To understand this text, readers need the following background knowledge.
Understanding of flat shapes versus 3-D shapes
Familiarity with a book's glossary
The ability to recognize objects in nature (like broccoli, the wildflower Queen Anne's lace, and bolts of lightning)

Explain	Before	During	After

	• Show everyday objects (either through a photo or the actual item) like the following:
	  • A fern leaf
	  • A head of broccoli
	  • A pineapple
	  • A pine cone
	• Lead students in a conversation about their observations of these items or photographs with these prompts:
	  • Describe the shapes you see
	  • What do you notice about these shapes?
	  • Comment about any patterns you see
		• Pages 4–7: Think aloud to highlight the photographs of shapes that are flat, and lines that are both straight and curved.
		• Pages 8–9: Clarify that these shapes in nature are not flat, but 3-D. Remind students they've previously explored how to determine calculations (like volume) for spheres and cylinders.
		• Page 12: Model how to synthesize key information (for example, "It's important for me to know that In 1975, Benoit Mandlebrot came up with the term fractals. Fractals occur in nature. They have patterns where the small part looks like the whole part; the small part is repeated over and over to make up the big object."
		• Pages 14–17: Have students turn and talk to a neighbor. Partner A tells partner B why broccoli is an example of a fractal. Partner B then explains why Queen Anne's lace is another example of a fractal.
		• Pages 18–21: Repeat the previous step, adding the examples of the patterns of lightning and rivers. Additionally, think aloud: "It's important for me to understand that fractals can keep the same shape as they add on, or that they can also change their shape the same way."
		• Pages 26–27: Ask students to clarify why caterpillars' markings are not fractals. Think aloud here by saying, "A key point here is that patterns in fractals are different sizes."
		• Pages 28–29: Ask students to think-pair-share. Ask, "Why are fractals useful in people's everyday lives? What do fractals in nature show people?"
			• Challenge students to bring in photographs or everyday objects that are fractals.
			• Read the book's afterword titled "The Boy Who Dreamed Up Fractals" by Michael Frame
			• Remind students about fractals through YouTube videos; search "Fun with Fractals" or BBC Ideas' (2019) "How Fractals Can Help You Understand the Universe"
			• Have students watch Ben Weiss's (2018) TED Talk titled "Fractals: A World in a Grain in Sand." Or have students view Benoit Mandelbrot's (2010) TED Talk titled "Fractals and the Art of Roughness"
			• Have students conduct internet searches for coloring sheets with fractals, or take pages out of Math Coloring Book: Fractals (Trube, 2018) for student use.

Engage and Extend	
	Use the book's glossary to clarify unfamiliar words. Team up with your school's art teacher to explore fractals in art. Team up with the science teacher to examine fractals in nature. Conduct research on where else people can observe fractals. Display fractal art (do a simple Google search). Did you know that much of the artwork of painter Jackson Pollock is considered fractal? (Visit www.fractalfoundation.org to learn more.)

Figure 4.5: Completed content-area read aloud planning template for *Mysterious Patterns: Finding Fractals in Nature* (Campbell, 2014).

Reading Aloud in Music

Though most secondary teachers report reading aloud frequently, those who do not are often teachers of elective courses such as physical education, art, and music (Ariail & Albright, 2006). However, opportunities abound to incorporate reading into these specialty areas. A music teacher might select from some of the fabulous picture book versions of popular songs. Did you know Twisted Sister, Bob Marley, Coldplay, and the Beach Boys are picture book authors? The following partial list includes picture books appropriate for all ages. Options are limitless! Secondary teachers grappling with social justice issues like Black Lives Matter and police violence might select lyrics from Bruce Springsteen's "41 Shots"—a perfect song to accompany popular young adult titles like *The Hate U Give* (Thomas, 2017). After all, song lyrics really are poetry in their rawest form, and poetry is best delivered through a read aloud.

- *Peace Train* (Stevens, 2021)
- *All You Need Is Love* (Lennon & McCartney, 2019)
- *Forever Young* (Dylan, 2008)
- *Respect* (Redding, 2020)
- *Good Vibrations* (Love & Wilson, 2020)
- *Get Up, Stand Up* (Marley, 2019)
- *Strawberry Swing* (Coldplay, 2021)

Here's a read aloud lesson based on the 2017 picture book *Imagine* (Lennon, 2017; see figure 4.6). Published in partnership with human rights organization Amnesty International, this picture book centers on a pigeon who flies around the world spreading a message of acceptance, compassion, and tolerance.

Beyond reading aloud texts derived from song lyrics, music teachers might include multiple texts they categorize according to various topics in music.

Show students that music is everywhere. Suggestions for early elementary grades books about the all-encompassing presence of music follow.

- *I Spy Music Everywhere* (Growing Kids Press, 2020)
- *Wild Symphony* (Brown, 2020)
- *Because* (Willems, 2019)
- *Never Play Music Right Next to the Zoo* (Lithgow, 2013)

Give students of all ages and grade levels a comprehensive sense of music. Text suggestions about the fundamentals of music follow.

- Wander around in the Dorling Kindersley (DK) compilation, *Music and How It Works: The Complete Guide for Kids* (Morland, 2020).
- Overview music history in *A History of Music for Children* (Richards & Schweitzer, 2021).

	Before	During	After
Evaluate		To understand this text, readers need the following background knowledge. The symbolism of olive branches as a sign of peace The understanding of conflict between countries The understanding that religions are also the source of many conflicts The meaning of greed	

Explain	• Don't play the musical version of the song.
	• Tell students you're going to read a book that presents the lyrics of a song, and their job is to determine the meaning of the lyrics and make some inferences about how the song might sound.
		• Think aloud at the following pausing points.
		• Pages 1-2: "I'm noticing this pigeon has a peace symbol on its bag and a branch in its mouth. I think it's an olive branch and it's a symbol of peace. This makes me think the pigeon is spreading messages of peace."
		• Pages 3-4: "I'm thinking the illustrator intentionally put the pigeon in the sky while the lyrics say sky."
		• Pages 7-8: "I'm getting the sense the author is asking me to imagine that if there were no countries, there might not be wars and conflicts between them—and that we'd all just see ourselves as people living together on the Earth."
		• Pages 9-10: "I'm noticing how many times the word imagine appears. It makes me think the writer wants me to envision or think about a world that is more peaceful."
		• Pages 13-14: "I'm getting the sense the author means that we are the people who want peace, who are dreamers about it."
		• Pages 15-16: "I'm noticing the pigeon—who is the spreader of peace—is hugging birds who look different (all shapes, sizes, and colors). Maybe that means the author also wants peace from people regardless of their color and size?"
		• Pages 21-22: "I see the words brotherhood of man. At first, I was confused since this only refers to boys or men, but I think the author actually means we all should get along more peacefully, and this doesn't have anything to do with gender."
		• Pages 23-24: "I notice the repetition of you may say I'm a dreamer. I think the author means people might think his idea of peace is impossible."
		• Pages 27-28: "This line shows me that we are all being invited into joining in peace. So the big idea here is we all can build peace."
			• Play the song once through.
			• Play the song while showing the lyrics.
			• Ask students the following questions to lead a conversation.
			  • "What is the tone of these lyrics? What mood do they set?"
			  • "What idea is the writer concerned about?"
			  • "How do the lyrics make you feel?"
			  • "Does the song make you aware of something you did not know before?"
			  • "Are there any surprises in the lyrics?"
			  • "What are the most important words to you? Why?"
			  • "What words or phrases are repeated? Why do you think the author might have done that?"

Engage and Extend		After playing the song for students, lead them in a conversation about their predictions of the music. Help them notice similarities and differences in what they predicted and how the music sounded. Ask them to reflect on how well the music and lyrics come together to set an overall tone, message, and mood for the piece.	

Figure 4.6: Completed content-area read aloud planning template for *Imagine* (Lennon, 2017).

Help students understand the role of instruments and how they come together. Text suggestions about the role of musical instruments follow.

- *88 Instruments* (Barton, 2016)
- *Clarinet and Trumpet* (Ellsworth, 2020)
- *Zin! Zin! Zin! A Violin* (Moss, 2005)
- *The Oboe Goes Boom Boom Boom* (Venable, 2020)

Show students the ways music informs social gatherings. Text suggestions featuring musical events (like the opera and concerts) follow.

- *The Dog Who Sang at the Opera* (Izen & West, 2004)
- *The Last Holiday Concert* (Clements, 2004)
- *The Piano Recital* (Miyakoshi, 2019)

Demonstrate to students the great diversity among musicians. Text suggestions of biographies follow.

- *Listen: How Evelyn Glennie, a Deaf Girl, Changed Percussion* (Stocker, 2022)
- *Trombone Shorty* (Andrews, 2015)
- *When Marian Sang: The True Recital of Marian Anderson* (Ryan, 2002)
- *Elvis Is King!* (Winter, 2019)
- *Nina: A Story of Nina Simone* (Todd, 2021)
- *Dancing Hands: How Teresa Carreño Played the Piano for President Lincoln* (Engle, 2019)

Showcase for students the significance and use of music throughout history. Text suggestions follow.

- *The President Sang Amazing Grace* (Mulford, 2019)
- *Like a Bird: The Art of the American Slave Song* (Grady, 2016)
- *What Was Woodstock?* (Holub, 2016)

Highlight for students the many forms music can take. Text suggestions follow.

- *The Roots of Rap: 16 Bars on the 4 Pillars of Hip-Hop* (Weatherford, 2019)
- *This Jazz Man* (Ehrhardt, 2006)
- *When the Beat Was Born: DJ Kool Herc and the Creation of Hip Hop* (Hill, 2013)
- *The History of Rock: For Big Fans and Little Punks* (Nabais, 2019)
- *Passing the Music Down* (Sullivan, 2011)

Finally, you might read aloud in upper-elementary and middle school classrooms from chapter books, where music plays a central role. Text suggestions follow.

- *The Chance to Fly* (Stroker & Davidowitz, 2021)
- *All Summer Long* (Larson, 2018)
- *Blackbird Fly* (Kelly, 2015)
- *Barakah Beats* (Siddiqui, 2021)

When you read aloud about music, you demonstrate its broadness, history, instrumentation, cultural significance, use of poetic form, and relevance to people's everyday lives.

Reading Aloud in Physical Education

Remember those physiological changes I discussed in chapter 1 (page 17)—that listening to someone reading improves heart rate and breathing for medically fragile babies (Campbell, 2019) and decreases pain for hospitalized children (Brockington et al., 2021)? If science indicates the body responds to listening to read alouds, teachers should incorporate read alouds into gym and physical education. I'm particularly fond of stories of athletes who overcome adversity, so the picture book memoir, *Fauja Singh Keeps Going: The True Story of the Oldest Person to Ever Run a Marathon* (Singh, 2020) captivated me immediately. It tells the true story of a Sikh man, Fauja Singh, who broke world records to become the first one-hundred-year-old to run a marathon. Moreover, it's the story of his grit and determination to overcome obstacles, and it provides important representation of the Sikh community. With a bit of preteaching some of the essential components of the protagonists' background and home, this story makes for a successful read aloud for early- and middle-elementary-grades readers. See figure 4.7 (page 90) for a content-area read aloud plan about this book.

Enjoy the true story of Fauja Singh? Discover more and read aloud from inspiring stories of athletes with disabilities, including the following titles.

- *No Barriers* series (https://12storylibrary.com/order-books/no-barriers-series-information; Perry, Mattern, & Ventura, 2020)

- *A Sporting Chance: How Ludwig Guttmann Created the Paralympic Games* (Alexander, 2020)

- *The William Hoy Story: How a Deaf Baseball Player Changed the Game* (Churnin, 2016)

- *Emmanuel's Dream: The True Story of Emmanuel Ofosu Yeboah* (Thompson, 2015)

For students in PreK–early elementary grades, read aloud from sports-related alphabet books. Here's a quick list of some text suggestions.

- Select any of the *Sports Alphabet* series (there are fifteen titles from Sleeping Bear Press), from *A Is for Axel: An Ice Skating Alphabet* (Browning, 2006) to *Z Is for Zamboni: A Hockey Alphabet* (Napier, 2002)

Just like there were no limits to Fauja's determination, there are no limits to how you might read aloud in physical education! Underpinning Singh's (2020) accomplishments is how sports unify and connect people globally, a theme that resonates in the following text suggestions for read alouds.

- *Sakamoto's Swim Club: How a Teacher Led an Unlikely Team to Victory* (Abery, 2021)

- *The Boys in the Boat: The True Story of an American Team's Epic Journey to Win Gold at the 1936 Olympics* (Brown, 2016).

Read aloud about sports in short bursts, from exciting sports clippings from newspapers featuring professional teams or local newspaper clippings featuring local student-athletes.

Evaluate

To understand this text, readers need the following background knowledge.

What a marathon is and its grueling nature	Vaisakhi: A festival during the harvest season
Cursory knowledge about Punjab	Traditional Punjab food, like daal and roti
A region in South Asia that wars divided to create India and Pakistan	Leaving home for the opportunities in another country
	London as a city in England
Punjab has own language, fashion, and music	Running as a form of exercise
Sikhism as the prominent religion of Punjab	Turbans as traditional Sikh headwear
Cricket, kites, and hopscotch as outdoor games	Why the New York City Marathon is an important and popular marathon
The challenges of not being able to walk	
Traveling on foot to a faraway school	Blisters as an impediment to running
Farming crops to provide for one's family	Prejudice or fear against Sikhs, particularly from Americans post-September 11, 2001

Explain

Before	During	After
• Have students draw a quick sketch of a runner. Ask them to describe their drawing to a neighbor. Brainstorm words they associate with runners, including words that come to mind when they run. • Show students the cover of the book. Ask them what they notice about the runner in the illustration and any similarities or differences between this image and their sketches. • Explain what a marathon is to students, including the distance of twenty-six miles and the length of time it takes an average runner to complete. You might show quick video explanations, from Encyclopedia Britannica (https://britannica.com/videos), Kiddle (https://kiddle.co), or YouTube Kids (https://youtube.com/channel/UCudZIfVvCSPMoVcqa7kxgGw). • Explain that the main character in the story is a Sikh man, who lives in an area called Punjab. Show a virtual map of Punjab. Point out that the man on the cover is wearing a turban and has a long beard, as a way to express his faith. • Listen to the correct pronunciation of the character's name (find it though a quick Google search).	• Page 3: Model a synthesis. "It's important for me to understand Fauja cannot walk, and people believe that he will never be able to walk." • Page 4: Explain that Sikh men don't cut their hair (or facial hair) as a way to show their faith. • Page 7: Ask students to generate words they associate with Fauja (like determined and hardworking). • Page 10: Ask students to give evidence from the book showing Fauja's determination and strong spirit. • Page 12: Model the author's purpose, explaining, "I'm noticing the words of encouragement Fauja gives his children are the same words he heard as a boy from his mother." • Page 16: Model synthesizing by saying, "The author wants me to understand Fauja moves to England to be closer to the family he missed." • Pages 17-18: Ask students to determine the mood of the illustrations. Ask, "How do you think Fauja feels in his new country?" • Page 22: Ask students to explain how running changes Fauja's mood. • Page 24: Have students recall their understanding of a marathon. • Page 26: Briefly explain why many Americans feared Sikhs after 9/11, and Fauja wanted to help people better understand his peaceful religion. • Page 28: Model author's purpose with a think aloud. "I'm noticing the words burst, pain, slow, exhausted, ambulance-all show me Fauja couldn't complete this marathon because of his fatigue and his painful blisters." • Pages 33-34: Ask students, "Why do you think the illustrations are depicted vertically rather than horizontally?"	Encourage discussions about how Fauja overcame adversity with the following prompts: • "How would you describe Fauja?" • "What are some of the challenges that he faced? How did he overcome these challenges?" • "What can we learn from his true story?" Connect Fauja's story to the sport of running through these conversation starters: • "Why was running so important in this book?" • "What is the significance of the New York City marathon for Fauja, particularly at this time in history?"

Engage and Extend	Read more on Fauja Singh on pages 35-36. Draw students' attention to the fact that the Guinness Book of World Records has yet to honor Fauja as the world's oldest marathoner because they are unwilling to accept his government's identification documents. Ask students what they think about this. Encourage them to write letters to the Guinness Book of World Records encouraging a change to this policy. Have students research the historical origins of marathons. Encourage students to research the principles of the Sikh religion, life in Punjab, or both. Show students interviews and videos of Fauja. Fauja says, "My secret to a long and healthy life has been taking care of my mind, body, and soul" (Singh, 2020, p. 46). Ask students to keep a log or list of the actions they do to take care of themselves. Lead students in researching other athletes who overcome physical and age limits to defy the odds in sports. Encourage students to investigate ageism and generate lists of examples.

Figure 4.7: Completed content-area read aloud planning template for *Fauja Singh Keeps Going* (Singh, 2020).

Prior to introducing a new sport or game, search for its rules, guidelines, and history (in resources like the National Association for Sport and Physical Education at https://pgpedia.com/n/national-association-sport-and-physical-education). Think aloud as you read the rules, being sure to model how you're visualizing and summarizing key ideas. National Geographic and Sports Illustrated also have a myriad of resources, including the following suggestions.

- *Big Book of WHO: All-Stars* (Editors of Sports Illustrated Kids, 2021)
- *Sports Illustrated Kids* magazine (see https://sikids.com/tag/magazine)
- Graphic novels, including *Spotlight Soccer* (Sanchez, 2015) and *Power at the Plate* (Ciencin, 2012)
- *Sports Illustrated Kids: Starting Line Readers* series (for beginning readers in the early elementary grades; Joven, 2017)
- *Weird but True! Sports: 300 Wacky Facts About Awesome Athletics* (National Geographic Kids, 2016)

Also consider reading aloud about more unusual sports, such as the following text suggestions.

- *Roller Derby Rivals* (Macy, 2014)
- *Skater Cielo* (Katstaller, 2022)
- *Annette Feels Free* (Mazeika, 2022)

Finally, read aloud from the following text suggestions to highlight for students how women fought for a role in sports.

- *An Equal Shot: How the Law Title IX Changed America* (Becker, 2021)
- *Miss Mary Reporting: The True Story of Sportswriter Mary Garber* (Macy, 2016)

Reading Aloud in the Arts

Opportunities abound to read aloud about art in PreK–8 classrooms. I was thrilled when my seventh-grade daughter told me each of her art classes begins with a read aloud. Her teacher selects a passage from *Harry Potter and the Sorcerer's Stone* (Rowling, 1998), reads aloud, and asks students to quickly sketch what they are hearing. The following sketch was her visualization of Harry Potter's cat-loving neighbor, Mrs. Figg (see figure 4.8). Similar to the visualization strategy from chapter 3 (page 59), students connect words and images to remind them of the power of descriptive language.

Source: Student work. Used with permission.

Figure 4.8: Student artwork.

Still, read alouds in art classes might be a challenge, given more limited time frames (after all, students do not typically visit art class every day), but they are nonetheless enjoyable and beneficial. To reduce students' anxiety about not being "good artists," for your read aloud, consider selecting a short picture book with an inspirational message that people are all good artists, as in the following example read aloud plan (see figure 4.9).

Need other art-inspired read alouds? Consider launching the school year with read alouds to remind students that art is expressive creativity, as author Tomie DePaola (1989) shows in *The Art Lesson,* Andrea Beaty (2021) in *Aaron Slater, Illustrator,* and Barney Saltzberg (2010) in *Beautiful Oops!* You might help students of all ages understand even artists were beginners with Elizabeth's Haidle's (2021) *Before They Were Artists: Famous Illustrators as Kids.*

		Before	During	After
Evaluate		To understand this text, readers need the following background knowledge. The inference of coloring outside the lines / How it feels to be embarrassed / The experience of learning from mistakes		

	Before	During	After

Explain	• Begin a discussion by asking juicy essential questions like, "Who are artists? What do artists do? What is the purpose of art?"
	
	 • Lead a conversation with students about learning from mistakes with the following questions: "Are mistakes a bad thing? What good things might come out of making a mistake?"
	
	 • If your students are independent writers, you might create a gallery walk. For this activity, display the preceding questions at a dedicated location and ask students to jot their responses on sticky notes (or using different colored markers).
		• Think aloud with the following prompts: "What is an artist?' I thought about it and what the inside cover said. The author is letting me know this whole book is his answer to that question."
		
		 • Page 3: "Artists try to see it all,' so the big idea here is artists are people who notice the beauty in our world."
		
		 • Page 7: "Things imagined and things she has seen.' This line lets me know art can come from real things and imaginary things."
		
		 • Page 8: "The artist plays with crayons, paint, and pencils.' I'm noticing the word plays . . . maybe the author is trying to tell me that art can be fun and not so serious."
		
		 • Page 9: "And so she must go on a journey far from home.' I'm thinking artists leave the safety of their homes to see more of the world and maybe to learn more."
		
		 • Page 13: ". . . for pictures!' This line makes me think the artist is feeling joy and excitement, mixed in with a little bit of nervousness."
		
		 • Page 18: ". . . so many people. All watching . . . All waiting." This line lets me know the artist feels nervous about showing her art to all these people."
		
		 • Page 20: "I think I've made a mistake.' I'm getting the sense the artist feels embarrassed of her art-she colored outside the lines and feels embarrassed."
		
		 • Page 24: "Mistakes are how you learn!' The author wants me to remember art doesn't have to be perfect. We learn from our mistakes, and mistakes are not a reason to stop doing something we love."
		
		 • Page 30: "So keep drawing because maybe you are an artist too!' The message of this book is people are all artists, even if they feel a bit scared to show their art and even if they feel like they made a mistake. The idea here is art makes people's hearts feel full."
			• Return to the original jottings (student responses) about the identity of artists, the purpose of art, and the role of mistakes. Encourage reflections and revisions including the following.
			
			  • "Does this book change your original thinking about who artists are?"
			
			  • "Does this book make you rethink the purpose of art?"
			
			  • "How does this book connect art and mistakes?"
			
			 • Encourage students to respond in conversation or writing to their initial thoughts from before the reading. You might have students respond to sentence starters like the following.
			
			  • "Artists are . . ."
			
			  • "Here's what people can learn from mistakes in their art . . ."
			
			  • "The reason people make art is . . ."

Engage and Extend	Research the author (and illustrator) Ed Vere and his work for BookTrust (https://booktrust.org.uk), his beliefs about children's books, and art. Find out what it means to be an artist in residence. Write a letter to a young artist to inspire the artist to keep making art. Talk to a neighbor about a time you made a mistake and learned from that mistake.

Figure 4.9: Completed content-area read aloud planning template for *The Artist* (Vere, 2023)

Crayons are a ubiquitous part of childhood, which is exactly the charm in the picture book biography, *The Crayon Man: The True Story of Crayola Crayons* (Biebow, 2019). Follow up with the fabulous *The Day the Crayons Quit* by Drew Daywalt (2013) and illustrated by Oliver Jeffers (and follow-up titles!). Students might explore color with Peter H. Reynolds's (2012) *Creatrilogy* box set (including my favorite, *Ish*), and *Mix It Up!* by Hervé Tullet (2014). I'm particularly fond of Penguin Random House's series, *What the Artist Saw* (Balkan, Guglielmo, Hodge, & Jackson, 2021–2022), which encourages students to unpack the art of Georgia O'Keefe, Faith Reingold, and others.

Just as my daughter's art class begins with a daily read aloud, so too might yours. Consider introducing An Artist a Day with brief biographies. Consider texts such as the following.

- *Artists and Their Pets: True Stories of Famous Artists and Their Animal Friends* (Hodge, 2017)
- *HerStory: 50 Women and Girls Who Shook Up the World* (Halligan, 2018)
- *Women in Art: 50 Fearless Creatives Who Inspired the World* (Ignotofsky, 2019)
- *Black Artists Shaping the World* (Jackson, 2021)

Upper-elementary and middle grade readers might enjoy read alouds that feature museums and or art-related mysteries. Consider the following texts.

- *From the Mixed-Up Files of Mrs. Basil E. Frankweiler* (Konigsburg, 2019)
- *Chasing Vermeer* (Balliett, 2004)
- *Many Points of Me* (Gertler, 2021)
- *The Lost Art Mysteries* series (Hicks, 2017–2021)
- *The Space Between Lost and Found* (Stark-McGinnis, 2020)
- *The Art of Running Away* (Kleckner, 2021)
- *The Frame-Up* (MacKnight, 2018)
- *Eddie Red Undercover: Mystery on Museum Mile* (Wells, 2014)

A Call to Action

This chapter invites all teachers—regardless of their content area—to push away the notion that read alouds only belong in the English language arts block. In fact, when teachers commit to reading aloud across all disciplines, they imbue their schools with a commitment to the power and richness of read alouds as a cornerstone of schoolwide literacy. The content-area read aloud might look different—it might occur in shorter bursts and from various genres and formats (including informational texts and primary documents)—but that's OK and even helpful. Reading aloud makes the often complex and dense material of content areas accessible and engaging to students. Every time teachers (those in art, physical education, music, science, mathematics, or social studies) read aloud, they send the message: literacy is a joyful element that unifies their school and deserves their time.

With so many engaging, diverse books on the market, it's overwhelming to stay on top of the breadth and depth of elementary and middle grades literature. To stay current, I highly recommend following your favorite professional organization (mine is the International Literacy Association at https://literacyworldwide.org) for recommended titles and award-winning children's books (see appendix D, page 109, for a compilation of these resources). In chapter 1 (page 17), I invited you to reflect on your own read aloud habits. My hunch is the majority of those read alouds did not occur in content-area classes, so now let content-area read alouds be your focus. Reflecting on the following questions may be useful.

- Think back to the last read aloud you did in a content area. What worked? What might you improve?

- How did you evaluate the frequency of your read alouds during content-area instruction?

- Did you write some goals for your inclusion of read alouds in content areas? Are these goals about frequency, the types of text, or your planning of the read aloud?

- What takeaways from this chapter might you share with a school-based colleague? Are there any particular nuggets to share with the electives teachers in your school building?

- Did you identify a content area where you could strengthen your read alouds? Did you select a book based on the instructional topic, and plan the read aloud with the template (see page 76)?

- Peruse the resources in appendix D (page 109). Which awards and compiled lists are new to you? How do you plan to make use of them?

- For a particular unit you're about to embark on, plan out your read alouds for that unit. What texts will you include?

- After reading aloud in content areas, reflect on students' reactions. What was their engagement or interest level?

Epilogue

I don't remember much about my first year of teaching, but it was 1999, and I was twenty-two years old. As a Teach For America corps member, I was placed in an East Oakland, California, middle school. Every day, I felt like I was in survival mode as I tried to meet the needs of students living in poverty, find teaching resources on a tight budget, and create a safe and welcoming classroom environment. I remember constant exhaustion, a chronic feeling of being overwhelmed, and also a tremendous sense of admiration for my students' perseverance and resilience. And of course, I remember laughter—as it's nearly impossible to not find humor in everyday middle school antics—kids really do say the darndest things! Eventually, after additional years of middle school teaching, I returned East to pursue my doctorate and become a professor.

Like every teacher, I frequently thought about what happened to my first group of students. I wondered how their remaining school years unfolded, how many had left East Oakland to pursue college, and what jobs and careers they pursued. I also realized it would be nearly impossible to track them down; I lost touch with so many of them and, at the time of my teaching, social media did not exist. In 1999, my cell phone was the size and weight of a brick, and in my first years of teaching, I didn't even have email!

Imagine my surprise in 2021 when I opened up my LinkedIn page to a request from a former student (I'll call Meuy). A message in my inbox read, "This is an odd message, but here it goes . . . I am reaching out to you because I am a former student of yours from Oakland, California, and want to connect. Do you remember me?"

Through grateful tears, I responded, "Of course I remember you. It is fabulous to hear from you." And I truly did remember Meuy; she was the youngest daughter of Cambodian immigrants, a diligent student with perfect handwriting and a serious work ethic. She was shy and sweet, spent her weekends at the local Buddhist community church, and frequently complimented my curly hair.

In corresponding emails, I discovered that Meuy had finished high school and attended the University of the Pacific, majoring in political science and minoring in prelaw. She was currently living in New Mexico and working in advertising. It was remarkable that after so many years and so many miles, she had tracked me down. Even more remarkable was a subsequent email she sent:

> Your classroom was almost like a "safe place," for me, so to speak. When you read us the book, *Crash*, it taught us patience and the ability to follow along and listen. I know there were so many more aspects to this but just to keep this short, I think you get my idea. THANK YOU. (Former student, personal communication, November 16, 2021)

More than twenty years later, this student remembered the title of my read aloud selection (I had definitely forgotten!). Although we studied ancient Mesopotamia, explored the origin of the Olympics, and covered the major civilizations through the fall of Rome, what stuck with Meuy over time was our shared read aloud.

I mention this example as a reminder of the power of read alouds, and while read alouds offer important academic benefits (as I've highlighted throughout this book), they also foster social-emotional connections, impart a love of reading, and transform classroom communities into more engaged, thoughtful, kind places.

A Final Call to Action

In writing this book, I had three overarching objectives.

1. To share out the compelling research and evidence revealing the myriad ways students benefit from read alouds

2. To advocate for daily read alouds from a wide repertoire of texts in all PreK–8 classrooms

3. To overview an easy-to-implement planning process to capitalize on instructional opportunities and head off potential comprehension challenges

My hope is this book either reaffirms, inspires, or invigorates you to consider how you incorporate read alouds into your routine instruction. Perhaps you are like Miss Viola Swamp from the introduction (page 1) and read alouds are the first thing to go when students are off task. Maybe you include read alouds a few times a week, either when time allows or as an incentive for students. It could be you are a middle school teacher who has never considered read alouds as a part of your instruction. Regardless of your starting point, I hope this book inspires forward motion for you in your read aloud instruction, either with a renewed sense of purpose, more intentional planning, or even a commitment to increase the frequency or duration of your read alouds. To promote that forward motion, I encourage your candid reflection (written, in a conversation with colleagues, or in a teacher book club) on these questions.

- What new takeaways emerged from this book?

- Consider your entry point to this book. What was your previous inclusion and planning of read alouds? Reflect on any way this book may shape or alter this.

- What portions of this book surprised you? Where did it challenge your thinking?

- What ideas and takeaways might you share with a school-based colleague?

- In what ways has this book impacted your future teaching?

- What are your students' reactions to your read alouds?

- Do you see student growth through read alouds? Comment on how.

- How might you encourage school leaders or colleagues to commit to and include read alouds in their instruction?

Let me close out with a reminder from an article in *American Educator*. Author Tanya S. Wright (2019) reminds teachers that "effective read-aloud techniques are purposeful and planned . . . effective interactive read-alouds can and should occur across the school day, in a broad range of content areas, and not just during language arts" (pp. 4–5).

Once teachers embrace the read aloud as an opportunity to build engagement, vocabulary, content knowledge, comprehension, motivation, and so many other academic and social-emotional skills, they increase students' development as readers, writers, and thinkers. Every PreK–8 teacher has the opportunity to do this every day, in every classroom.

APPENDIX A

Planning Templates

Read Aloud Planning Template

Title of Text:

<table>
<tr><td rowspan="4">Evaluate</td><td colspan="4">Background Knowledge</td></tr>
<tr><td colspan="4">Funds of Knowledge</td></tr>
<tr><td colspan="4">Potential Stumbling Blocks</td></tr>
<tr><td colspan="4">Instructional Opportunities</td></tr>
</table>

<table>
<tr>
<td rowspan="11">Explain</td>
<td colspan="4">Brainstorm Unfamiliar Words</td>
</tr>
<tr>
<th>Words to Teach</th>
<th>Short, Simple, Straightforward Definitions</th>
<th>Words to Explain</th>
<th>Short, Simple, Straightforward Definitions</th>
</tr>
<tr><td></td><td></td><td></td><td></td></tr>
<tr><td></td><td></td><td></td><td></td></tr>
<tr><td></td><td></td><td></td><td></td></tr>
<tr><td></td><td></td><td></td><td></td></tr>
<tr><td></td><td></td><td></td><td></td></tr>
<tr><td colspan="4">Think Alouds</td></tr>
<tr><td colspan="2">Stopping or Pausing Points</td><td colspan="2">I Language</td></tr>
</table>

<table>
<tr><td rowspan="3">Engage and Extend</td><td>Social-Emotional Learning Engagement</td></tr>
<tr><td>Cross-Curricular Extensions</td></tr>
<tr><td>Extensions to Support Reading and Writing</td></tr>
</table>

Planning Template for Content-Area Read Alouds

Evaluate	To understand this text, readers need the following background knowledge.

	Before	During	After
Explain			

Engage and Extend	

Resources for Content-Area Read Alouds

Resources for Reading Aloud in Social Studies

- Scott O'Dell Award for Historical Fiction (https://scottodell.com/the-scott-odell-award)

- The New York Historical Society Children's History Book Prize (https://nyhistory.org/about/childrens-history-book-prize)

- American Indian Youth Literature Award (https://ailanet.org/activities/american-indian-youth-literature-award)

- Jane Addams Children's Book Awards (https://janeaddamschildrensbookaward.org)

- Arab American Book Award (https://arabamericanmuseum.org/book-awards)

- Orbis Pictus Award (https://ncte.org/awards/orbis-pictus-award-nonfiction-for-children)

- Middle East Book Award (www.meoc.us/book-awards.html)

- Notable Books for a Global Society (www.clrsig.org/nbgs-lists.html)

- Carter G. Woodson Book Awards (https://socialstudies.org/membership/awards/carter-g-woodson-book-awards)

- Inspired Inner Genius books (https://toppsta.com/books/series/50124/inspired-inner-genius)

Resources for Reading Aloud in Science

- The AAAS/Subaru SB&F Prize for Excellence in Science Books (www. sbfprize.org)

- The Royal Society's Young People's Book Prize (https://royalsociety.org/ grants-schemes-awards/book-prizes/young-peoples-book-prize/)

- The American Phytopathological Society's De Bary Award for Outstanding Children's Science Books

- Outstanding Science Trade Books for Students from the National Science Teaching Association

Resources for Reading Aloud in Mathematics

- Read Aloud Revival's *Podcast #147: Our Favorite Math Read Alouds* (https:// readaloudrevival.com/147-2)

- Math Read Aloud Books (https://goodreads.com/shelf/show/math-read-alouds)

- Math: Our Favorite Picture Book Read Alouds (https://www.booklovefamily. com/p/math-picture-books.html) from Book Love Family

- 12 Picture Books by Mighty Girls Who Love Math (https://www.amightygirl. com/blog?p=20118)

- 40 Children's Books That Foster a Love of Math (https://dreme.stanford.edu/ news/40-childrens-books-that-foster-a-love-of-math/)

- 21 Most Beautifully Illustrated Math Books for Kids (https://ali.medium. com/14-beautifully-illustrated-childrens-books-for-early-math-learning-331d7bfd9fa6)

- (Award-winning) Books for Kids (https://www.mathicalbooks.org/)

Resources for
Choosing Read Aloud Titles

With so many fabulous books constantly coming out, it's daunting to stay on top of everything. These resources will be helpful in text selection.

Websites

- We Need Diverse Books (WNDB; https://diversebooks.org)
- The Brown Bookshelf (https://thebrownbookshelf.com)
- Unite Against Book Bans (https://uniteagainstbookbans.org)
- What Do We Do All Day (https://whatdowedoallday.com)
- Rebel Girls (https://rebelgirls.com)
- A Mighty Girl (https://amightygirl.com)
- Jon Scieszka's Guys Read (https://jonscieszka.com/guys-read)
- Read Aloud 15 MINUTES (https://readaloud.org)
- The Children's Book Council (https://cbcbooks.org)
- Penguin Random House's Brightly (https://readbrightly.com)
- IndieBound (https://indiebound.org/kids-indie-next-list)

Podcasts

- *Yarn: A Story Podcast* (https://yarnpodcast.com)
- *Read Aloud Revival* (https://readaloudrevival.com)
- *All the Wonders* (https://www.allthewonders.com/podcasts/)

- *Picturebooking* (https://picturebooking.com)
- *Curious City* (https://curiouscitydpw.com)
- *What Should I Read Next? With Anne Bogel* (https://modernmrsdarcy.com/what-should-i-read-next/)
- *The Guardian Children's Book Podcast* (https://www.theguardian.com/childrens-books-site/series/childrens-books-podcast)

Professional Organizations and Journals

- *The Horn Book Magazine* (www.hbook.com)
- American Library Association (https://ala.org)
- American Association of School Librarians (https://ala.org/aasl)
- *Bookology* (https://www.bookologymagazine.com/)
- National Council of Teachers of English (https://ncte.org)
- International Literacy Association (https://literacyworldwide.org)
- National Association for the Education of Young Children (NAEYC; https://naeyc.org)

Lists of Children's Book Awards

General Awards

- Great Graphic Novels for Teens Committee list compiled annually by a committee of the Young Adult Library Services Association (YALSA; www.ala.org/yalsa/booklistsawards/booklists/greatgraphicnovelsforteens/policies)

- Alex Awards administered by YALSA to honor the top ten adult books published during the previous year with appeal to readers between the ages of twelve and eighteen (https://ala.org/yalsa/alex-awards)

- Randolph Caldecott Medal annually recognizes the preceding year's "most distinguished American picture book for children" (https://ala.org/alsc/awardsgrants/bookmedia/Caldecott)

- John Newbery Medal given by the Association for Library Service to Children, a division of the American Library Association, to the author of "the most distinguished contributions to American literature for children" (https://ala.org/alsc/awardsgrants/bookmedia/newbery)

- William C. Morris Award honors a book written for young adults by a first-time, previously unpublished author (https://ala.org/yalsa/morris-award)

- Michael L. Printz Award for Excellence in Young Adult Literature presented annually by the Young Adult Library Services Association to honor the best book written for teens, based entirely on its literary merit (https://ala.org/yalsa/printz)

- Boston Globe–Horn Book Awards given by *The Boston Globe* and *The Horn Book Magazine* for outstanding fiction or poetry, outstanding nonfiction, and outstanding illustration (https://hbook.com/page/boston-globe-horn-book-awards-landing-page)

Diversity Awards

- Rainbow Book List (https://glbtrt.ala.org/rainbowbooks/archives/1429) recommends titles for youth from birth to age eighteen that contain significant and authentic gay, lesbian, bisexual, transgender, queer, or questioning (LGBTQIA+) content.

- The Sibert Medal is awarded annually to the writer and illustrator of the most distinguished informational book published in English during the preceding year (https://maag.guides.ysu.edu/childrensbookawards/sibert).

- The YALSA Award for Excellence in Nonfiction for Young Adults honors the best nonfiction book published for young adults (https://www.ala.org/yalsa/nonfiction).

- Rise: A Feminist Book Project List is sponsored by the Feminist Task Force of the Social Responsibilities Round Table of the American Library Association, which selects a list of recommended feminist books, fiction and nonfiction, for young readers from preschool through age eighteen (https://www.ala.org/rt/2022-rise-feminist-book-project-list).

- Coretta Scott King Book Awards are given annually to outstanding African American authors and illustrators of books for children and young adults that demonstrate an appreciation of African American culture and universal human values (https://ala.org/rt/cskbart).

- The Pura Belpré Award honors a Latino or Latina writer and illustrator whose work best portrays, affirms, and celebrates the Latino cultural experience in an outstanding work of literature for children and youth (https://www.ala.org/alsc/awardsgrants/bookmedia/belpre).

- The Stonewall Book Award is a set of three literary awards that annually recognize "exceptional merit relating to the gay/lesbian/bisexual/transgender experience" (https://ala.org/rt/rrt/award/stonewall/honored).

- Asia/Pacific American Librarians Association Literature (APALA) Awards are given to honor and recognize individual work about Asian/Pacific Americans and their heritage, based on literary and artistic merit (https://www.apalaweb.org/awards/literature-awards/).

- Sydney Taylor Book Awards are presented annually to outstanding books for children and teens that authentically portray the Jewish experience (https://jewishlibraries.org/stba-about).

- Native American Youth Services Awards are given by the American Indian Library Association (AILA) to identify and honor the best writing and illustrations by and about American Indians (https://ailanet.org/activities/american-indian-youth-literature-award/).

Awards for Books in Social Studies

- Scott O'Dell Award for Historical Fiction (https://scottodell.com/the-scott-odell-award)

- The New York Historical Society Children's History Book Prize (https://nyhistory.org/about/childrens-history-book-prize)

- American Indian Youth Literature Award (https://ailanet.org/activities/american-indian-youth-literature-award)

- Jane Addams Children's Book Awards (https://janeaddamschildrensbookaward.org)

- Arab American Book Award (https://arabamericanmuseum.org/book-awards)

- Orbis Pictus Award (https://ncte.org/awards/orbis-pictus-award-nonfiction-for-children)

- Middle East Book Award (www.meoc.us/book-awards.html)

- Notable Books for a Global Society (www.clrsig.org/nbgs-lists.html)

- Carter G. Woodson Book Awards (https://socialstudies.org/membership/awards/carter-g-woodson-book-awards)

Awards for Books in Science

- The AAAS/Subaru SB&F Prize for Excellence in Science Books (www.sbfprize.org)

- The Royal Society's Young People's Book Prize (https://royalsociety.org/grants-schemes-awards/book-prizes/young-peoples-book-prize)

- The American Phytopathological Society's De Bary Award for Outstanding Children's Science Books (https://apsnet.org/edcenter/resources/Pages/DeBary.aspx)

- Outstanding Science Trade Books for Students from the National Science Teaching Association (https://nsta.org/outstanding-science-trade-books-students-k-12)

Further Reading

The following list includes some of my favorite books, which I use to select children's books, create read aloud instructional routines, and encourage parents or caregivers to continue reading aloud at home.

Ahiyya, V. (2022). *Rebellious read alouds: Inviting conversations about diversity with children's books, grades K–5*. Thousand Oaks, CA: Corwin Press.

Bellingham, R. L. (2019). *The artful read-aloud: 10 principles to inspire, engage, and transform learning*. Portsmouth, NH: Heinemann.

Gurdon, M. C. (2019). *The enchanted hour: The miraculous power of reading aloud in the age of distraction*. New York: Harper.

Hintz, A., & Smith, A. T. (2021). *Mathematizing children's literature: Sparking connections, joy, and wonder through read-alouds and discussion*. Portsmouth, NH: Stenhouse.

Layne, S. L. (2015). *In defense of read-aloud: Sustaining best practice*. Portland, ME: Stenhouse.

Rajan, R. S. (2022). *The read aloud factor: How to create the habit that boosts your baby's brain*. Chicago: Parenting Press.

Walther, M. (2019). *The ramped-up read aloud: What to notice as you turn the page*. Thousand Oaks, CA: Corwin Literacy.

Children's Books Cited

Abery, J. (2021). *Sakamoto's swim club: How a teacher led an unlikely team to victory* (C. Sasaki, Illus.). Toronto, Ontario, Canada: Kids Can Press.

Aggs, P. (2021). *It's her story Shirley Chisholm* (M Jenai, Illus.). Chicago: Sunbird Books.

Ahmed, R. (2018). *Mae among the stars* (S. Burrington, Illus.). New York: Harper.

Alexander, L. (2020). *A sporting chance: How Ludwig Guttmann created the Paralympic Games* (A. Drummond, Illus.). Boston: Houghton Mifflin Harcourt.

Allard, H. (1977). *Miss Nelson is missing!* (J. Marshall, Illus.). Boston: Houghton Mifflin.

Andrews, T. (2015). *Trombone Shorty* (B. Collier, Illus.). New York: Abrams Books for Young Readers.

Armand, G. (2021). *Black leaders in the civil rights movement: A Black history book for kids* (M. Perera, Illus.). Emeryville, CA: Rockridge Press.

Avery, B. P. (2022). *Black men in science: A Black history book for kids* (N. Leanne, Illus.). Emeryville, CA: Rockridge Press.

Balkan, G., Guglielmo, A., Hodge, S., & Jackson, S. (2021–2022). *What the artist saw* (J. Bloggs, K. Ekdahl, & A. Pippins, Illus.). New York: Dorling Kindersley (DK).

Balliett, B. (2004). *Chasing Vermeer* (B. Helquist, Illus.). New York: Scholastic Press.

Barretta, G. (2020). *The secret garden of George Washington Carver* (F. Morrison, Illus.). New York: Tegen Books.

Barton, B. (2019). *I'm trying to love math* (B. Barton, Illus.). New York: Viking.

Barton, C. (2016). *88 instruments* (L. Thomas, Illus.). New York: Knopf.

Beason, J. (2021). *Native Americans in history: A history book for kids* (A. Lenz, Illus.). Emeryville, CA: Rockridge Press.

Beaty, A. (2016). *Ada Twist, scientist* (D. Roberts, Illus.). New York: Abrams Books for Young Readers.

Beaty, A. (2021). *Aaron Slater, illustrator* (D. Roberts, Illus.). New York: Abrams Books for Young Readers.

Becker, H. (2020). *Emily Noether: The most important mathematician you've never heard of* (K. Rust, Illus.). Toronto, Ontario, Canada: Kids Can Press.

Becker, H. (2021). *An equal shot: How the law Title IX changed America* (D. Phumiruk, Illus.). New York: Holt.

Bolden, T. (2022). *Speak up, speak out! The extraordinary life of fighting Shirley Chisholm.* Washington, DC: National Geographic.

Brooks, B. (2018). *Stories for boys who dare to be different: True tales of amazing boys who changed the world without killing dragons* (Q. Winter, Illus.). New York: Running Press Kids.

Brown, D. (2020). *Wild symphony* (S. Batori, Illus.). New York: Rodale Kids.

Brown, D. J. (2016). *The boys in the boat: The true story of an American team's epic journey to win gold at the 1936 Olympics.* New York: Puffin Books.

Brown, M. (2018). *Frida Kahlo and her animalitos* (J. Parra, Illus.). Holland, OH: Dreamscape Media.

Brown, T. F. (2022). *Not done yet: Shirley Chisholm's fight for change* (N. Crews, Illus.). Minneapolis, MN: Millbrook Press.

Browning, K. (2006). *A is for axel: An ice skating alphabet* (M. Rose, Illus.). Chelsea, MI: Sleeping Bear Press.

Buckley, J., Jr. (2017). *Who are Venus and Serena Williams?* (A. Thomson, Illus.). New York: Penguin.

Buckley, J., Jr. (2020). *It's a numbers game! Basketball: The math behind the perfect bounce pass, the buzzer-beating bank shot, and so much more!* Washington, DC: National Geographic.

Bunting, P. (2023). *The gentle genius of trees.* New York: Crown Books.

Burnell, C. (2020). *I am not a label: 34 disabled artists, thinkers, athletes and activists from past and present* (L. Baldo, Illus.). Beverly, MA: Wide Eyed Editions.

Calkhoven, L. (2021). *Shirley Chisholm* (K. S. O'Connor, Illus.). New York: Stevens.

Campbell, S. C. (2014). *Mysterious patterns: Finding fractals in nature.* Honesdale, PA: Boyds Mills Press.

Campoy, F. I., & Howell, T. (2019). *Maybe something beautiful: How art transformed a neighborhood* (T. López, Illus.). Holland, OH: Dreamscape Media.

Carle, E. (1997). *From head to toe.* New York: HarperCollins.

Chambers, V. (2020). *Shirley Chisholm is a verb* (R. Baker, Illus.). New York: Dial Books for Young Readers.

Chisholm, S. (2020). *Shirley Chisholm: The last interview and other conversations.* New York: Melville House.

Cho, T. (2022). *Asian American women in science: An Asian American history book for kids* (M. D. Perera, Illus.). Oakland, CA: Rockridge Press.

Churnin, N. (2016). *The William Hoy story: How a deaf baseball player changed the game* (J. Tuya, Illus.). Chicago: Whitman.

Ciencin, S. (2012). *Power at the plate* (Z. Huerta, A. Bracho, & F. Cano, Illus.). North Mankato, MN: Stone Arch Books.

Claybourne, A. (2019). *I can be a math magician* (K. Kear, Illus.). Mineola, NY: Dover.

Cleary, B. P. (2005–2014). *Math is CATegorical* (B. Gable, Illus.). Minneapolis, MN: Millbrook Press.

Clements, A. (1996). *Frindle* (B. Selznick, Illus.). New York: Atheneum Books for Young Readers.

Clements, A. (2004). *The last holiday concert.* New York: Simon & Schuster.

Clinton, C. (2017). *She persisted: 13 American women who changed the world* (A. Boiger, Illus.). New York: Philomel Books.

Coldplay. (2021). *Strawberry swing* (M. Miller, Illus.). New York: Akashic Books.

Davis, B. F., & Mubeen, J. (2020). *What's the point of math?* (C. Hassan, Illus.). New York: Dorling Kindersley (DK).

Day, C. (2021). *Maria Tallchief* (G. Flint, Illus.). New York: Philomel Books.

Daywalt, D. (2013). *The day the crayons quit* (O. Jeffers, Illus.). New York: Philomel Books.

de la Peña, M. (2021). *Milo imagines the world* (C. Robinson, Illus.). New York: Putnam's.

Demi. (1997). *One grain of rice: A mathematical folktale*. New York: Scholastic Press.

DePaola, T. (1989). *The art lesson*. New York: Putnam.

Dufresne, E. (2021a). *Sports*. New York: Booklife.

Dufresne, E. (2021b). *STEM*. New York: Booklife.

Dylan, B. (2008). *Forever young* (P. Rogers, Illus.). New York: Atheneum Books.

Editors of Sports Illustrated Kids. (2021). *Big book of who: All-stars*. Chicago: Triumph Books.

Ehrhardt, K. (2006). *This jazz man* (R. G. Roth, Illus.). Orlando, FL: Harcourt.

Ellsworth, M. (2020). *Clarinet and trumpet* (J. Herzog, Illus.). Boston: Clarion Books.

Engle, M. (2019). *Dancing hands: How Teresa Carreño played the piano for President Lincoln* (R. López, Illus.). New York: Atheneum Books for Young Readers.

Fabiny, S. (2022). *Who was Georgia O'Keeffe?* (D. Putra, Illus.). New York: Penguin.

Faruqi, S., & Mumtaz, A. (2022). *The wonders we seek: 30 incredible Muslims who helped shape the world* (S. Khan, Illus.). New York: Quill Tree Books.

Favilli, E., & Cavallo, F. (2016–2022). *Good night stories for rebel girls*. Larkspur, CA: Rebel Girls.

Feiner, B. (2019). *Sports women legends alphabet*. Bradford, CT: Alphabet.

Fletcher, T., & Rue, G. (2021). *Wonder women of science: 12 geniuses who are currently rocking science, technology, and the world* (S. W. Comport, Illus.). Somerville, MA: Candlewick Press.

Floca, B. (2003). *The racecar alphabet*. New York: Atheneum Books for Young Readers.

Frazee, M. (2003). *Roller coaster*. San Diego, CA: Harcourt.

Gertler, C. (2021). *Many points of me* (V. Stamper, Illus.). New York: Greenwillow Books.

Grady, C. (2016). *Like a bird: The art of the American slave song* (M. Wood, Illus.). Minneapolis, MN: Millbrook Press.

Grady, C. (2018). *Write to me: Letters from Japanese American children to the librarian they left behind* (A. Hirao, Illus.). Watertown, MA: Charlesbridge.

Growing Kids Press. (2020). *I spy music everywhere: A fun alphabet guessing game book for kids ages 2–5*. Author.

Guglielmo, A., & Tourville, J. (2017). *Pocket full of colors: The magical world of Mary Blair, Disney artist extraordinaire* (B. Barrager, Illus.). New York: Atheneum Books for Young Readers.

Haidle, E. (2021). *Before they were artists: Famous illustrators as kids*. New York: Houghton Mifflin Harcourt.

Halligan, K. (2018). *HerStory: 50 women and girls who shook up the world* (S. Walsh, Illus.). New York: Simon & Schuster Books for Young Readers.

Halls, K. M. (2022). *Famous artists in history: 15 painters, sculptors, and photographers you should know* (A. Blackwell, Illus.). Oakland, CA: Rockridge Press.

Harrison, V. (2017–2019). *Little leaders*. New York: Little, Brown.

Harvey, J. W. (2022). *Ablaze with color: A story of painter Alma Thomas* (L. Wise, Illus.). New York: HarperCollins.

Her Majesty Queen Rania Al Abdullah, & DiPucchio, K. (2010). *The sandwich swap* (T. Tusa, Illus.). New York: Disney-Hyperion Books.

Hicks, D. (2017–2021). *The lost art mysteries* series. New York: Clarion Books.

Hill, L. C. (2013). *When the beat was born: DJ Kool Herc and the creation of hip hop* (T. Taylor, Illus.). New York: Roaring Brook Press.

Hinton, S. E. (1967). *The outsiders*. New York: Penguin.

Hodge, S. (2017). *Artists and their pets: True stories of famous artists and their animal friends* (V. Lemay, Illus.). New York: Duo Press.

Holub, J. (2016). *What was Woodstock?* (G. Copeland, Illus.). New York: Grosset & Dunlap.

Hughes, K. (2020). *Displacement*. New York: First Second.

Ignotofsky, R. (2017). *Women in sports: 50 fearless athletes who played to win*. New York: Ten Speed Press.

Ignotofsky, R. (2019). *Women in art: 50 fearless creatives who inspired the world*. New York: Ten Speed Press.

Izen, M., & West, J. (2004). *The dog who sang at the opera* (E. Oller, Illus.). New York: Abrams.

Jackson, S. (2021). *Black artists shaping the world*. London: Thames & Hudson.

Joven, C. C. (2017). *Sports Illustrated Kids: Starting line readers* series (E. Shems, & A. López, Illus.). North Mankato, MN: Stone Arch Books.

Kato, J. E. (2012). *Manuel's murals* (R. Smith, Illus.). Sacramento, CA: 3L.

Kay, A. (2020). *Kay's anatomy: A complete (and completely disgusting) guide to the human body* (H. Paker, Illus.). New York: Delacorte Press.

Keating, J. (2016). *Pink is for blobfish: Discovering the world's perfectly pink animals* (D. DeGrand, Illus.). New York: Knopf.

Keating, J. (2019). *Gross as a snot otter: Discovering the world's most disgusting animals* (D. DeGrand, Illus.). New York: Knopf.

Keating, J. (2021). *Big as a giant snail: Discovering the world's most gigantic animals* (D. DeGrand, Illus.). New York: Knopf.

Kelly, E. E. (2015). *Blackbird fly*. New York: Greenwillow Books.

Kleckner, S. (2021). *The art of running away*. Mendota Heights, MN: Jolly Fish Press.

Konigsburg, E. L. (2019). *From the mixed-up files of Mrs. Basil E. Frankweiler*. New York: Atheneum Books for Young Readers.

LaBarge, M. (2020). *Women artists A to Z* (C. Corrigan, Illus.). New York: Dial Books for Young Readers.

Lapin, J. (2019). *If you had your birthday party on the moon* (S. Ceccarelli, Illus.). New York: Sterling Children's Books.

Larson, H. (2018). *All summer long*. New York: Farrar, Straus & Giroux.

Lee-Tai, A. (2006). *A place where sunflowers grow* (F. Hoshino, Illus.). New York: Children's Book Press.

Lennon, J., & McCartney, P. (2019). *All you need is love* (M. Rosenthal, Illus.). New York: Little Simon.

Levinson, C. (2021). *The people's painter: How Ben Shahn fought for justice with art* (E. Turk, Illus.). New York: Abrams Books for Young Readers.

Lithgow, J. (2013). *Never play music right next to the zoo* (L. Hernandez, Illus.). New York: Simon & Schuster Books for Young Readers.

Littlejohn, J. (2018). *B is for baller: The ultimate basketball alphabet* (M. Shipley, Illus.). Chicago: Triumph Books.

Littlejohn, J. (2019). *G is for golazo: The ultimate soccer alphabet* (M. Shipley, Illus.). Chicago: Triumph Books.

Love, M. (2016). *Good vibrations: My life as a Beach Boy*. New York: Blue Rider Press.

Love, M., & Wilson, B. (2020). *Good vibrations* (P. Hoppe, Illus.). New York: Akashic Books.

MacKnight, W. M. (2018). *The frame-up*. New York: Greenwillow Books.

Macy, S. (2014). *Roller derby rivals* (M. Collins, Illus.). New York: Holiday.

Macy, S. (2016). *Miss Mary reporting: The true story of sportswriter Mary Garber* (C. F. Payne, Illus.). New York: Simon & Schuster Books for Young Readers.

Marley, C. (2019). *Get up, stand up* (J. J. Cabuay, Illus.). San Francisco: Chronicle Books.

Meltzer, B. (2014–2023). *Ordinary people change the world* (C. Eliopoulos, Illus.). New York: Penguin.

Miranda, A. (2019). *Tangled: A story about shapes* (E. Comstock, Illus.). New York: Simon & Schuster Books for Young Readers.

Miyakoshi, A. (2019). *The piano recital.* Toronto, Ontario, Canada: Kids Can Press.

Mochizuki, K. (1993). *Baseball saved us* (D. Lee, Illus.). New York: Lee & Low Books.

Morland, C. (2020). *Music and how it works: The complete guide for kids* (D. Humphries, Illus.). New York: Dorling Kindersley (DK).

Mosca, J. F. (2017). *The girl who thought in pictures: The story of Dr. Temple Grandin* (D. Rieley, Illus.). Seattle, WA: Innovation Press.

Mosca, J. F. (2018). *The girl with a mind for math: The story of Raye Montague* (D. Rieley, Illus.). Seattle, WA: Innovation Press.

Moss, L. (2005). *Zin! Zin! Zin! A violin* (M. Priceman, Illus.). New York: Aladdin.

Moss, M. (2013). *Barbed wire baseball: How one man brought hope to the Japanese internment camps of WWII* (Y. Shimizu, Illus.). New York: Abrams Books for Young Readers.

Mulford, Z. (2019). *The president sang Amazing Grace* (J. Scher, Illus.). Petaluma, CA: Cameron Kids.

Nabais, R. (2019). *The history of rock: For big fans and little punks* (J. Raimundo, Illus.). Chicago: Triumph Books.

Napier, M. (2002). *Z is for Zamboni: A hockey alphabet* (M. Rose, Illus.). Chelsea, MI: Sleeping Bear Press.

National Geographic Kids. (2016). *Weird but true! Sports: 300 wacky facts about awesome athletics.* Washington, DC: National Geographic.

Neuschwander, C., Einhorn, E., Kroll, V., & Sparagna LoPresti, A. (1997–2014). *Charlesbridge math adventures* (W. Geehan, D. Clark, P. O'Neill, & P. Hornung, Illus.). Watertown, MA: Charlesbridge.

Nichols, D. (2021). *Art of protest: Creating, discovering, and activating art for your revolution* (D. Dagadita, S. Saddo, O. Twist, M. Mendoza, & D. Becas, Illus.). Somerville, MA: Candlewick Press.

Paul, R. (2011). *Stomp!* New York: Scholastic.

Paulsen, G. (1999). *Hatchet.* New York: Aladdin.

Pellum, K. B. (2019). *Black women in science: A Black history book for kids* (K. Morris, Illus.). Emeryville, CA: Rockridge Press.

Pinkney, A. D. (2021). *Harriet Tubman* (G. Flint, Illus.). New York: Philomel Books.

Rebel Girls. (2021). *Rebel Girls champions: 25 tales of unstoppable athletes.* Larkspur, CA: Author.

Redding, O. (2020). *Respect* (R. Moss, Illus.). New York: Akashic Books.

Reid, M. (2021). *Maryam's magic: The story of mathematician Maryam Mirzakhani* (A. Jaleel, Illus.). New York: Balzer and Bray.

Reynolds, P. H. (2012). *Creatrilogy.* Somerville, MA: Candlewick Press.

Reynoso, N. (2021). *Courageous history makers: 11 women from Latin America who changed the world* (J. Leal, Illus.). Los Angeles: Con Todo Press.

Rhee, H. K. (2020). *The paper kingdom* (P. Campion, Illus.). New York: Random House.

Richards, M., & Schweitzer, D. (2021). *A history of music for children* (R. Blake, Illus.). New York: Thames & Hudson.

Riley, S. (2021). *The floating field: How a group of Thai boys built their own soccer field* (N. Quang, & K. Lien, Illus.). Minneapolis, MN: Millbrook Press.

Robeson, T. (2019). *Queen of physics: How Wu Chien Shiung helped unlock the secrets of the atom* (R. Huang, Illus.). New York: Sterling.

Rocco, J. (2020). *How we got to the moon: The people, technology, and daring feats of science behind humanity's greatest adventure.* New York: Crown Books for Young Readers.

Rosenstock, B. (2017). *Vincent can't sleep: Van Gogh paints the night sky* (M. GrandPré, Illus.). New York: Knopf.

Russell-Brown, K. (2020). *She was the first! The trailblazing life of Shirley Chisholm* (E. Velasquez, Illus.). New York: Lee & Low Books.

Ryan, P. M. (1999). *Amelia and Eleanor go for a ride* (B. Selznick, Illus.). New York: Scholastic Press.

Ryan, P. M. (2002). *When Marian sang: The true recital of Marian Anderson* (B. Selznick, Illus.). New York: Scholastic Press.

Sachar, L. (2001). *Holes.* New York: Dell Laurel-Leaf Books.

Saltzberg, B. (2010). *Beautiful oops!* New York: Workman.

Sanchez, R. (2015). *Spotlight soccer* (I. Waryanto, Illus.). North Mankato, MN: Stone Arch Books.

Scott, J., Spangler, B., & Sweet, M. (2021). *Unbound: The life + art of Judith Scott* (M. Sweet, Illus.). New York: Knopf.

Shetterly, M. L. (2018). *Hidden figures: The true story of four Black women and the space race* (L. Freeman, Illus.). New York: Harper.

Siddiqui, M. (2021). *Barakah beats.* New York: Scholastic.

Singh, S. J. (2020). *Fauja Singh keeps going: The true story of the oldest person to ever run a marathon* (B. Kaur, Illus.). New York: Kokila.

Solis, N. (2021). *The color collector* (R. Metallinou, Illus.). Ann Arbor, MI: Sleeping Bear Press.

Stabler, D. (2016). *Kid artists: True tales of childhood from creative legends* (D. Horner, Illus.). Philadelphia: Quirk Books.

Stark-McGinnis, S. (2020). *The space between lost and found.* New York: Bloomsbury.

Steig, W. (1986). *Brave Irene.* New York: Farrar, Straus & Giroux.

Steig, W. (1998). *Pete's a pizza.* New York: HarperCollins.

Stevens, C. (2021). *Peace train* (P. H. Reynolds, Illus.). New York: Harper.

Stocker, S. (2022). *Listen: How Evelyn Glennie, a deaf girl, changed percussion* (S. Holzwarth, Illus.). New York: Dial Books.

Stroker, A., & Davidowitz, S. (2021). *The chance to fly.* New York: Amulet Books.

Stuart, C. (2019). *The language of the universe: A visual exploration of mathematics* (X. Abadía, Illus.). Somerville, MA: Big Picture Press.

Sullivan, S. (2011). *Passing the music down* (B. Root, Illus.). Somerville, MA: Candlewick Press.

Takei, G., Eisinger, J., & Scott, S. (2020). *They called us enemy* (H. Becker, Illus.). San Diego, CA: Top Shelf.

Tang, G. (2001). *The grapes of math: Mind stretching math riddles* (H. Briggs, Illus.). New York: Scholastic.

Thimmesh, C. (2018). *Girls think of everything: Stories of ingenious inventions by women* (M. Sweet, Illus.). Boston: Houghton Mifflin.

Thimmesh, C. (2022). *Girls solve everything: Stories of women entrepreneurs building a better world* (M. Sweet, Illus.). Boston: Houghton Mifflin.

Thomas, A. (2017). *The hate u give.* New York: Balzer and Bray.

Thompson, L. A. (2015). *Emmanuel's dream: The true story of Emmanuel Ofosu Yeboah* (S. Qualls, Illus.). New York: Schwartz & Wade Books.

Todd, T. N. (2021). *Nina: A story of Nina Simone* (C. Robinson, Illus.). New York: Putnam's.

Todd, T. N. (2022). *Holding her own: The exceptional life of Jackie Ormes* (S. Wright, Illus.). New York: Orchard Books.

Tokuda-Hall, M. (2022). *Love in the library* (Y. Imamura, Illus.). Somerville, MA: Candlewick Press.

Torres, J. (2021). *Stealing home* (D. Namisato, Illus.). Toronto, Ontario, Canada: Kids Can Press.

Trusty, K. (2021). *Black inventors: 15 inventions that changed the world* (J. Polk, Illus.). Emeryville, CA: Rockridge Press.

Tullet, H. (2014). *Mix it up!* San Francisco: Handprint Books.

Van Dusen, C. (2009). *The circus ship*. Somerville, MA: Candlewick Press.

Venable, C. A. F. (2020). *The oboe goes boom boom boom* (L. Cho, Illus.). New York: Greenwillow Books.

Verde, S. (2018). *Hey, wall: A story of art and community* (J. Parra, Illus.). New York: Simon & Schuster Books for Young Readers.

Vergara, M. I. S. (2016–2023). *Little people, big dreams* series. London: Frances Lincoln Children's Books.

Wade, J. (2021). *Nano: The spectacular science of the very (very) small* (M. Castrillón, Illus.). Somerville, MA: Candlewick Press.

Wallmark, L. (2017). *Grace Hopper: Queen of computer code* (K. Wu, Illus.). New York: Sterling Children's Books.

Wang, A. (2021). *Watercress* (J. Chin, Illus.). New York: Porter Books.

Wargin, K. (2004). *M is for melody: A music alphabet* (K. Larson, Illus.). Chelsea, MI: Sleeping Bear Press.

Warhola, J. (2003). *Uncle Andy's: A faabbbulous visit with Andy Warhol*. New York: Putnam's.

Weatherford, C. B. (2019). *The roots of rap: 16 bars on the 4 pillars of hip-hop* (F. Morrison, Illus.). New York: Little Bee Books.

Wells, M. (2014). *Eddie Red undercover: Mystery on Museum Mile* (M. Calo, Illus.). Boston: Houghton Mifflin Harcourt.

Weltman, A. (2021). *The book of math: Adventures in the world of shapes and numbers* (P. Boston, Illus.). Tulsa, OK: Kane Miller Books.

White, E. B. (1952). *Charlotte's web* (G. Williams, Illus.). New York: Harper.

Willems, M. (2004). *Knuffle Bunny: A cautionary tale*. New York: Hyperion Books for Children.

Willems, M. (2019). *Because* (A. Ren, Illus.). New York: Hyperion Books for Children.

Williams, A. D. (2021). *Shirley Chisholm dared: The story of the first Black woman in Congress* (A. Harrison, Illus.). New York: Schwartz Books.

Winter, J. (2017). *The world is not a rectangle: A portrait of architect Zaha Hadid*. New York: Beach Lane Books.

Winter, J. (2019). *Elvis is king!* (Red Nose Studio, Illus.). New York: Schwartz & Wade Books.

Woo, E. (2019). *It's a numberful world: How math is hiding everywhere*. New York: The Experiment.

Woodward, C. V. (2022). *Family dynamics: Embrace your sound* (T. Vu, Illus.). Four Hearts Books.

Yamasaki, K., & Lender, I. (2020). *Everything Naomi loved* (K. Yamasaki, Illus.). New York: Norton Young Readers.

Yang, K. (2022). *Yes we will: Asian Americans who shaped this country* (N. H. Ali, F. Azim, M. Chin, S. Deng, S. Gupta, J. Kuo, et al., Illus.). New York: Dial Books for Young Readers.

Zuckerman, G. (2016). *Rising above: How 11 athletes overcame challenges in their youth to become stars*. New York: Philomel Books.

References and Resources

Abery, J. (2021). *Sakamoto's swim club: How a teacher led an unlikely team to victory* (C. Sasaki, Illus.). Toronto, Ontario, Canada: Kids Can Press.

Adamson, T. K. (2011a). *Basketball: The math of the game.* North Mankato, MN: Capstone Press.

Adamson, T. K. (2011b). *Baseball: The math of the game.* North Mankato, MN: Capstone Press.

Aggs, P. (2021). *It's her story Shirley Chisholm* (M. Jenai, Illus.). Chicago: Sunbird Books.

Ahiyya, V. (2022). *Rebellious read alouds: Inviting conversations about diversity with children's books, grades K–5.* Thousand Oaks, CA: Corwin Press.

Ahmed, R. (2018). *Mae among the stars* (S. Burrington, Illus.). New York: Harper.

Albright, L. K. (2002). Bringing the Ice Maiden to life: Engaging adolescents in learning through picture book read-alouds in content areas. *Journal of Adolescent and Adult Literacy, 45*(5), 418–428.

Alexander, A. (1960). The gray flannel cover on the American history textbook. *Social Education, 24*, 11–14.

Alexander, L. (2020). *A sporting chance: How Ludwig Guttmann created the Paralympic Games* (A. Drummond, Illus.). Boston: Houghton Mifflin Harcourt.

Allard, H. (1977). *Miss Nelson is missing!* (J. Marshall, Illus.). Boston: Houghton Mifflin.

Allington, R. L. (2014). Reading moves: What not to do. *Educational Leadership, 72*(2), 16–21.

Anderson, P. (2022). *APA cites 12-percent 2020 US audiobook revenue growth.* Accessed at https://publishingperspectives.com/2021/06/audio-publishers-association-12-percent-audiobook -revenue-growth-in-2020-covid19/ on May 16, 2023.

Anderson, R. C. (1984). Role of the reader's schema in comprehension, learning, and memory. In R. C. Anderson, J. Osborn, & R. J. Tierney (Eds.), *Learning to read in American schools: Basal readers and content texts* (pp. 243–258). Hillsdale, NJ: Erlbaum.

Anderson, R. C., Hiebert, E. H., Scott, J. A., & Wilkinson, I. A. G. (1985). *Becoming a nation of readers: The report of the commission on reading.* Washington, DC: The National Institute of Education.

Andrews, T. (2015). *Trombone Shorty* (B. Collier, Illus.). New York: Abrams Books for Young Readers.

Ariail, M., & Albright, L. K. (2006). A survey of teachers' read-aloud practices in middle schools. *Reading Research and Instruction, 45*(2), 69–89.

Armand, G. (2021). *Black leaders in the civil rights movement: A Black history book for kids* (M. Perera, Illus.). Emeryville, CA: Rockridge Press.

Artley, A. S. (1975). Good teachers of reading: Who are they? *The Reading Teacher, 29*(1), 26–31.

Avery, B. P. (2022). *Black men in science: A Black history book for kids* (N. Leanne, Illus.). Emeryville, CA: Rockridge Press.

Baker, D. L., Mogna, V., Rodriguez, S., Farmer, D., & Yovanoff, P. (2016). Building the oral language of young Hispanic children through interactive read alouds and vocabulary games at preschool and at home. *Journal of International Special Needs Education, 19*(2), 81–94.

Balkan, G., Guglielmo, A., Hodge, S., & Jackson, S. (2021–2022). *What the artist saw* (J. Bloggs, K. Ekdahl, & A. Pippins, Illus.). New York: Dorling Kindersley (DK).

Balliett, B. (2004). *Chasing Vermeer* (B. Helquist, Illus.). New York: Scholastic Press.

Barretta, G. (2020). *The secret garden of George Washington Carver* (F. Morrison, Illus.). New York: Tegen Books.

Barton, B. (2019). *I'm trying to love math* (B. Barton, Illus.). New York: Viking.

Barton, C. (2016). *88 instruments* (L. Thomas, Illus.). New York: Knopf.

Baumann, J. F., Jones, L. A., & Seifert-Kessell, N. (1993). Using think alouds to enhance children's comprehension monitoring abilities. *The Reading Teacher, 47*(3), 184–193.

BBC Ideas. (2019). *How fractals can help you understand the universe* [Video file]. Accessed at https://youtube.com/watch?v=w_MNQBWQ5DI on February 6, 2023.

Beason, J. (2021). *Native Americans in history: A history book for kids* (A. Lenz, Illus.). Emeryville, CA: Rockridge Press.

Beaty, A. (2016). *Ada Twist, scientist* (D. Roberts, Illus.). New York: Abrams Books for Young Readers.

Beaty, A. (2021). *Aaron Slater, illustrator* (D. Roberts, Illus.). New York: Abrams Books for Young Readers.

Beck, I. L., & McKeown, M. G. (2001). Text talk: Capturing the benefits of read-aloud experiences for young children. *The Reading Teacher, 55*(1), 10–20.

Beck, I. L., McKeown, M. G., & Kucan, L. (2013). *Bringing words to life: Robust vocabulary instruction.* New York: Guilford Press.

Becker, H. (2020). *Emily Noether: The most important mathematician you've never heard of* (K. Rust, Illus.). Toronto, Ontario, Canada: Kids Can Press.

Becker, H. (2021). *An equal shot: How the law Title IX changed America* (D. Phumiruk, Illus.). New York: Holt.

Bellingham, R. L. (2019). *The artful read-aloud: 10 principles to inspire, engage, and transform learning.* Portsmouth, NH: Heinemann.

Bennett, C. (2020, February 12). *ELL students' background knowledge as an academic fund.* Accessed at https://thoughtco.com/ell-students-funds-of-knowledge-4011987 on January 31, 2023.

Bensel, L. (2023). Interdisciplinary read alouds: Building background knowledge to support learning across science and social studies. *Michigan Reading Journal, 55*(3).

Bereiter, C., & Bird, M. (1985). Use of thinking aloud in identification and teaching of reading comprehension strategies. *Cognition and Instruction, 2*(2), 131–156.

Berkeley, S., & Larsen, S. (2018). Fostering self-regulation of students with learning disabilities: Insights from 30 years of reading comprehension intervention research. *Learning Disabilities Research and Practice, 33*(2), 75–86.

Best, E., Clark, C., & Picton, I. (2020). *Children, young people and audiobooks before and during lockdown.* London: National Literacy Trust. Accessed at https://files.eric.ed.gov/fulltext/ED607856.pdf on January 31, 2023.

Biber, D., & Conrad., S. (2019). *Register, genre, and style* (2nd ed.). Cambridge, England: Cambridge University Press.

Biebow, N. (2019). *The crayon man: The true story of the invention of Crayola Crayons* (S. Salerno, Illus.). Boston: Houghton Mifflin Harcourt.

Biemiller, A. (2010). *Words worth teaching: Closing the vocabulary gap.* Columbus, OH: McGraw-Hill Science Research Associates (SRA).

Bingham, G. E., Venuto, N., Carey, M., & Moore, C. (2018). Making it REAL: Using informational picture books in preschool classrooms. *Early Childhood Education Journal, 46*(5), 467–475.

Blewitt, P., & Langan, R. (2016). Learning words during shared book reading: The role of extratextual talk designed to increase child engagement. *Journal of Experimental Child Psychology*, 150, 404–410. Accessed at https://doi.org/10.1016/j.jecp.2016.06.009 on July 14, 2023.

Block, C. C., & Israel, S. E. (2004). The ABCs of performing highly effective think-alouds. *The Reading Teacher, 58*(2), 154–167.

Bocala, C., McMaken, J., & Melchior, K. (2019). *Evaluating the use of EL education's K–2 language arts curriculum.* Accessed at https://files.eleducation.org/web/downloads/Evaluating-the-Use-of-EL-Education%E2%80%99s-K-2-Language-Arts-Curriculum-Feb-2021.pdf on June 19, 2023.

Bolden, T. (2022). *Speak up, speak out! The extraordinary life of fighting Shirley Chisholm.* Washington, DC: National Geographic.

BrainyQuote. (n.d.a). *Amelia Earhart quotes.* Accessed at https://brainyquote.com/authors/amelia-earhart-quotes on February 3, 2023.

BrainyQuote. (n.d.b). *Eleanor Roosevelt quotes.* Accessed at https://www.brainyquote.com/authors/eleanor-roosevelt-quotes on February 3, 2023.

Brannon, D., & Dauksas, L. (2014). The effectiveness of dialogic reading in increasing English language learning preschool children's expressive language. *International Research in Early Childhood Education, 5*(1), 1–10.

Braun, P. (2010). Taking the time to read aloud. *Science Scope, 34*(2), 45–49.

Britt, S., Wilkins, J., Davis, J., & Bowlin, A. (2016). The benefits of interactive read-alouds to address social-emotional learning in classrooms for young children. *Journal of Character Education, 12*(2), 43–57.

Brockington, G., Moreira, A. P. G., Buso, M. S., da Silva, S. G., Altszyler, E., Fischer, R., et al. (2021). Storytelling increases oxytocin and positive emotions and decreases cortisol and pain in hospitalized children. *Psychological and Cognitive Sciences, 118*(22), 1–7. Accessed at https://doi.org/10.1073/pnas.2018409118 on July 14, 2023.

Broemmel, A. D., Rearden, K. T., & Buckner, C. (2021). Teachers' choices: Are they the right books for science instruction? *The Reading Teacher, 75*(1), 7–16.

Brooks, B. (2018). *Stories for boys who dare to be different: True tales of amazing boys who changed the world without killing dragons* (Q. Winter, Illus.). New York: Running Press Kids.

Brown, D. (2020). *Wild symphony* (S. Batori, Illus.). New York: Rodale Kids.

Brown, D. J. (2016). *The boys in the boat: The true story of an American team's epic journey to win gold at the 1936 Olympics.* New York: Puffin Books.

Brown, M. (2018). *Frida Kahlo and her animalitos* (J. Parra, Illus.). Holland, OH: Dreamscape Media.

Brown, T. F. (2022). *Not done yet: Shirley Chisholm's fight for change* (N. Crews, Illus.). Minneapolis, MN: Millbrook Press.

Browning, K. (2006). *A is for axel: An ice skating alphabet* (M. Rose, Illus.). Chelsea, MI: Sleeping Bear Press.

Buckley, J., Jr. (2017). *Who are Venus and Serena Williams?* (A. Thomson, Illus.). New York Penguin.

Buckley, J., Jr. (2020). *It's a numbers game! Basketball: The math behind the perfect bounce pass, the buzzer-beating bank shot, and so much more!* Washington, DC: National Geographic.

Bunting, P. (2023). *The gentle genius of trees.* New York: Crown Books.

Burnell, C. (2020). *I am not a label: 34 disabled artists, thinkers, athletes and activists from past and present* (L. Baldo, Illus.). Beverly, MA: Wide Eyed Editions.

Cabell, S. Q., & Hwang, H. (2020). Building content knowledge to boost comprehension in the primary grades. *Reading Research Quarterly, 55*(S1), S97–S107. Accessed at https://doi.org/10.1002/rrq.338 on July 14, 2023.

Caldwell, J., & Leslie, L. (2010). Thinking aloud in expository text: Processes and outcomes. *Journal of Literacy Research, 42*(3), 308–340.

Calkhoven, L. (2021). *Shirley Chisholm* (K. S. O'Connor, Illus.). New York: Stevens.

Campbell, D. (2019, April 26). *How reading to NICU babies can help moms in a big way.* Accessed at https://www.mother.ly/parenting/how-reading-to-nicu-baby-can-help-moms-too/ on January 31, 2023.

Campbell, S. C. (2014). *Mysterious patterns: Finding fractals in nature.* Honesdale, PA: Boyds Mills Press.

Campoy, F. I., & Howell, T. (2019). *Maybe something beautiful: How art transformed a neighborhood* (T. López, Illus.). Holland, OH: Dreamscape Media.

Carle, E. (1997). *From head to toe.* New York: HarperCollins.

Catts, H. W. (2022). Rethinking how to promote reading comprehension. *American Educator, 45*(4), 26–33.

Cervetti, G. N., & Wright, T. S. (2020). The role of knowledge in understanding and learning from text. In E. B. Moje, P. P. Afflerbach, P. Enciso, & N. K. Lesaux (Eds.), *Handbook of Reading Research* (Vol. V, pp. 237–260). New York: Taylor & Francis.

Cervetti, G. N., Barber, J., Dorph, R., Pearson, P. D., & Goldschmidt, P. G. (2012). The impact of an integrated approach to science and literacy in elementary school classrooms. *Journal of Research in Science Teaching, 49*(5), 631–658.

Chambers, V. (2020). *Shirley Chisholm is a verb* (R. Baker, Illus.). New York: Dial Books for Young Readers.

Chin, C., & Osborne, J. (2008). Students' questions: A potential resource for teaching and learning science. *Studies in Science Education, 44*(1), 1–39.

Chin, C., Brown, D. E., & Bruce, B. C. (2002). Student-generated questions: A meaningful aspect of learning in science. *International Journal of Science Education, 24*(5), 521–549.

Chisholm, S. (2020). *Shirley Chisholm: The last interview and other conversations.* New York: Melville House.

Cho, T. (2022). *Asian American women in science: An Asian American history book for kids* (M. D. Perera, Illus.). Oakland, CA: Rockridge Press.

Chouinard, M. M., Harris, P. L., & Maratsos, M. P. (2007). Children's questions: A mechanism for cognitive development. *Monographs of the Society for Research in Child Development, 72*(1), I, v, vii–ix, 1–129.

Churnin, N. (2016). *The William Hoy story: How a deaf baseball player changed the game* (J. Tuya, Illus.). Chicago: Whitman.

Ciencin, S. (2012). *Power at the plate* (Z. Huerta, A. Bracho, & F. Cano, Illus.). North Mankato, MN: Stone Arch Books.

Clark, S. K., & Andreasen, L. (2014). Examining sixth grade students' reading attitudes and perceptions of teacher read aloud: Are all students on the same page? *Literacy Research and Instruction, 53*(2), 162–182.

Clark R. C. (2007). *Audiobooks for children: Is this really reading?* Accessed at http://interactivereadalouds.pbworks.com/f/Audiobooks+for+Children+-+Is+this+Really+Reading.pdf on May 1, 2023.

Claybourne, A. (2019). *I can be a math magician* (K. Kear, Illus.). Mineola, NY: Dover.

Cleary, B. P. (2005–2014). *Math is CATegorical* (B. Gable, Illus.). Minneapolis, MN: Millbrook Press.

Clements, A. (1996). *Frindle* (B. Selznick, Illus.). New York: Atheneum Books for Young Readers.

Clements, A. (2004). *The last holiday concert.* New York: Simon & Schuster.

Clinton, C. (2017). *She persisted: 13 American women who changed the world* (A. Boiger, Illus.). New York: Philomel Books.

Clinton, V. (2019). Reading from paper compared to screens: A systematic review and meta-analysis. *Journal of Research in Reading, 42*(2), 288–325.

Coiro, J. (2011). Talking about reading as thinking: Modeling the hidden complexities of online reading comprehension. *Theory Into Practice, 50*(2), 107–115.

Coiro, J., & Dobler, E. (2007). Exploring the online reading comprehension strategies used by sixth-grade skilled readers to search for and locate information on the internet. *Reading Research Quarterly, 42*(2), 214–257.

Coldplay. (2021). *Strawberry swing* (M. Miller, Illus.). New York: Akashic Books.

Collaborative for Academic, Social, and Emotional Learning. (n.d.a). *Fundamentals of SEL.* Accessed at https://casel.org/fundamentals-of-sel on January 31, 2023.

Collaborative for Academic, Social, and Emotional Learning. (n.d.b). *What is the CASEL framework?* Accessed at https://casel.org/fundamentals-of-sel/what-is-the-casel-framework/#responsible on January 31, 2023.

Costello, B., & Kolodziej, N. J. (2006). A middle school teacher's guide for selecting picture books. *Middle School Journal, 38*(1), 29–33.

Cunningham, A. E., & Stanovich, K. E. (1997). Early reading acquisition and its relation to reading experience and ability 10 years later. *Developmental Psychology, 33*(6), 934–945.

Davis, B. F., & Mubeen, J. (2020). *What's the point of math?* (C. Hassan, Illus.). New York: Dorling Kindersley (DK).

Dawson, N., Hsiao, Y., Tan, A. W. M., Banerji, N., & Nation, K. (2021). Features of lexical richness in children's books: Comparisons with child-directed speech. *Language Development Research, 1*(1), 9–53.

Day, C. (2021). *Maria Tallchief* (G. Flint, Illus.). New York: Philomel Books.

Daywalt, D. (2013). *The day the crayons quit* (O. Jeffers, Illus.). New York: Philomel Books.

DeJulio, S., Martinez, M., Harmon, J., Wilburn, M., & Stavinoha, M. (2022). Read aloud across grade levels: A closer look. *Literacy Practice and Research, 47*(2). Accessed at https://digitalcommons.fiu.edu/cgi/viewcontent.cgi?article=1019&context=lpr on January 31, 2023.

de la Peña, M. (2021). *Milo imagines the world* (C. Robinson, Illus.). New York: Putnam's.

Demi. (1997). *One grain of rice: A mathematical folktale.* New York: Scholastic Press.

DePaola, T. (1989). *The art lesson.* New York: Putnam.

Di Teodoro, S., Donders, S., Kemp-Davidson, J., Robertson, P., & Schuyler, L. (2011). Asking good questions: Promoting greater understanding of mathematics through purposeful teacher and student questioning. *The Canadian Journal of Action Research, 12*(2), 18–29.

Dohms, E. (2019, January 25). *No, listening to audiobooks isn't cheating, professor says.* Accessed at https://wpr.org/no-listening-audiobooks-isnt-cheating-professor-says on September 19, 2022.

Dorl, J. (2007). Think aloud! Increase your teaching power. *Young Children, 62*(4), 101–105.

Dowdall, N., Melendez-Torres, G. J., Murray, L., Gardner, F., Hartford, L., & Cooper, P. J. (2020). Shared picture book reading interventions for child language development: A systematic review and meta-analysis. *Child Development, 91*(2). Accessed at https://doi.org/10.1111/cdev.13225 on July 14, 2023.

Dufresne, E. (2021a). *Sports.* New York: Booklife.

Dufresne, E. (2021b). *STEM*. New York: Booklife.

Duke, N. K. (2000). 3.6 minutes per day: The scarcity of informational texts in first grade. *Reading Research Quarterly, 35*(2), 202–224.

Duke, N. K., Ward, A. E., & Pearson, P. D. (2021). The science of reading comprehension instruction. *The Reading Teacher, 74*(6), 663–672.

Duncan, D. (1978). *What classroom observations reveal about reading comprehension instruction* (Technical Report No. 106). Washington, DC: National Institute of Education.

Durkin, D. (1978). What classroom observation reveals about reading comprehension instruction. *Reading Research Quarterly, 14*(4), 481–533.

Dwyer, M., & Martin-Chang, S. (2023). Fact from fiction: The learning benefits of listening to historical fiction. *The Reading Teacher*. Accessed at https://doi.org/10.1002/trtr.21.77 on July 14, 2023.

Dylan, B. (2008). *Forever young* (P. Rogers, Illus.). New York: Atheneum Books.

Dymock, S. (2007). Comprehension strategy instruction: Teaching narrative text structure awareness. *The Reading Teacher, 61*(2), 161–167.

Editors of Sports Illustrated Kids. (2021). *Big book of who: All-stars*. Chicago: Triumph Books.

Ehrhardt, K. (2006). *This jazz man* (R. G. Roth, Illus.). Orlando, FL: Harcourt.

Ellsworth, M. (2020). *Clarinet and trumpet* (J. Herzog, Illus.). Boston: Clarion Books.

Engle, M. (2019). *Dancing hands: How Teresa Carreño played the piano for President Lincoln* (R. López, Illus.). New York: Atheneum Books for Young Readers.

Evans, M., Williamson, K., & Pursoo, T. (2008). Preschoolers' attention to print during shared book reading. *Scientific Studies of Reading, 12*(1), 106–129.

Fabiny, S. (2022). *Who was Georgia O'Keeffe?* (D. Putra, Illus.). New York: Penguin.

Faruqi, S., & Mumtaz, A. (2022). *The wonders we seek: 30 incredible Muslims who helped shape the world* (S. Khan, Illus.). New York: Quill Tree Books.

Favilli, E., & Cavallo, F. (2016–2022). *Good night stories for rebel girls*. Larkspur, CA: Rebel Girls.

Feiner, B. (2019). *Sports women legends alphabet*. Branford, CT: Alphabet.

First Book. (n.d.). *Literacy rich classroom library checklist*. Accessed at https://firstbook.org/solutions/literacy-rich-classrooms/on May 3, 2023.

Fisher, D., Flood, J., Lapp, D., & Frey, N. (2004). Interactive read-alouds: Is there a common set of implementation practices? *The Reading Teacher, 58*(1), 8–17.

Fisher, D., Frey, N., & Hattie, J. (2017). *Teaching literacy in the visible learning classroom*. Thousand Oaks, CA: Corwin Literacy.

Fitchett, P. G., Heafner, T., & VanFossen, P. J. (2014). An analysis of time prioritization for social studies in elementary school classrooms. *Journal of Curriculum and Instruction, 8*(2), 7–35.

Fletcher, T., & Rue, G. (2021). *Wonder women of science: 12 geniuses who are currently rocking science, technology, and the world* (S. W. Comport, Illus.). Somerville, MA: Candlewick Press.

Floca, B. (2003). *The racecar alphabet*. New York: Atheneum Books for Young Readers.

Flynn, K. S. (2011). Developing children's oral language skills through dialogic reading: Guidelines for implementation. *Teaching Exceptional Children, 44*(2), 8–16.

Fontana, S. (Writer). (2012). In Nee, C., O'Connell, D., & Gaffney, C. (Executive Producers), *Doc McStuffins* [Television series]. Burbank, CA: Disney Junior.

Frazee, M. (2003). *Roller coaster*. San Diego, CA: Harcourt.

Frazier, B. N., Gelman, S. A., & Wellman, H. M. (2009). Preschoolers search for explanatory information within adult-child conversation. *Child Development, 80*(6), 1592–1611.

Frederick, S. G. (2011a). *Football: The math of the game*. North Mankato, MN: Capstone Press.

Frederick, S. G. (2011b). *Hockey: The math of the game*. North Mankato, MN: Capstone Press.

Gertler, C. (2021). *Many points of me* (V. Stamper, Illus.). New York: Greenwillow Books.

Gewertz, C. (2020, June 29). *Survey of mostly-white educators finds 1 in 5 think textbooks accurately reflect people of color*. Accessed at https://www.edweek.org/teaching-learning/survey-of-mostly -white-educators-finds-1-in-5-think-textbooks-accurately-reflect-people-of-color/2020/06on January 31, 2023.

Ghaith, G., & Obeid, H. (2004). Effect of think alouds on literal and higher-order reading comprehension. *Educational Research Quarterly, 27*(3), 49–57.

Gibbs, A. S., & Reed, D. K. (2023). Shared reading and science vocabulary for kindergarten students. *Early Childhood Education Journal, 51*(1), 127–138.

Giles, R., & Morrison, K. (2023). An investigation of Prekindergarten teachers' read aloud choices. *Literacy Practice and Research, 48*(2).

Gillies, R. M., Nichols, K., Burgh, G., & Haynes, M. (2014). Primary students' scientific reasoning and discourse during cooperative inquiry-based science activities. *International Journal of Educational Research, 63*, 127–140. Accessed at https://doi.org/10.1016/j.ijer.2013.01.001 on July 14, 2023.

Giroir, S., Grimaldo, L. R., Vaughn, S., & Roberts, G. (2015). Interactive read-alouds for English learners in the elementary grades. *The Reading Teacher, 68*(8), 639–648.

González, N., Moll, L. C., & Amanti, C. (Eds.). (2005). *Funds of knowledge: Theorizing practices in households, communities, and classrooms*. New York: Routledge.

Goodreads. (n.d.). *Emelia Earhart quotes*. Accessed at https://www.goodreads.com/quotes/tag/amelia -earhart on February 3, 2023.

Grady, C. (2016). *Like a bird: The art of the American slave song* (M. Wood, Illus.). Minneapolis, MN: Millbrook Press.

Grady, C. (2018). *Write to me: Letters from Japanese American children to the librarian they left behind* (A. Hirao, Illus.). Watertown, MA: Charlesbridge.

Graesser, A. C., & Person, N. K. (1994). Question asking during tutoring. *American Educational Research Journal, 31*(1), 104–137. Accessed at https://doi.org/10.2307/1163269 on July 14, 2023.

Graham, S., Bollinger, A., Booth Olson, C., D'Aoust, C., MacArthur, C., McCutchen, D., et al. (2012). *Teaching elementary school students to be effective writers: A practice guide*. Washington, DC: National Center for Education Evaluation and Regional Assistance, Institute of Education Sciences, U. S. Department of Education.

Gray, A. M., Sirinides, P. M., Fink, R. E., & Bowden, A. B. (2022) Integrating literacy and science instruction in kindergarten: Results from the efficacy study of *Zoology One. Journal of Research on Educational Effectiveness, 15*(1), 1–27. Accessed at https://doi.org/10.1080/19345747.2021.1938313 on July 14, 2023.

Growing Kids Press. (2020). *I spy music everywhere: A fun alphabet guessing game book for kids ages 2–5*. Author.

Grysko, R. A., & Zygouris-Coe, V. I. (2020). Supporting disciplinary literacy and science learning in grades 3–5. *The Reading Teacher, 73*(4), 485–499.

Guglielmo, A., & Tourville, J. (2017). *Pocket full of colors: The magical world of Mary Blair, Disney artist extraordinaire* (B. Barrager, Illus.). New York: Atheneum Books for Young Readers.

Gurdon, M. C. (2019). *The enchanted hour: The miraculous power of reading aloud in the age of distraction*. New York: Harper.

Hadley, E. B., & Mendez, K. Z. (2021). Learning words that matter: Selecting vocabulary words for young children. *The Reading Teacher, 74*(5), 595–605.

Haidle, E. (2021). *Before they were artists: Famous illustrators as kids*. New York: Houghton Mifflin Harcourt.

Halligan, K. (2018). *HerStory: 50 women and girls who shook up the world* (S. Walsh, Illus.). New York: Simon & Schuster Books for Young Readers.

Halls, K. M. (2022). *Famous artists in history: 15 painters, sculptors, and photographers you should know* (A. Blackwell, Illus.). Oakland, CA: Rockridge Press.

Harrison, V. (2017–2019). *Little leaders*. New York: Little, Brown.

Harvey, J. W. (2022). *Ablaze with color: A story of painter Alma Thomas* (L. Wise, Illus.). New York: HarperCollins.

Harvey, S., & Goudvis, A. (2007). *Strategies that work: Teaching comprehension for understanding and engagement* (2nd ed.). Portland, ME: Stenhouse.

Hedges, H., Cullen, J., & Jordan, B. (2011). Early years curriculum: Funds of knowledge as a conceptual framework for children's interests. *Journal of Curriculum Studies, 43*(2), 185–205.

Her Majesty Queen Rania Al Abdullah. (2010). *The sandwich swap* (T. Tusa, Illus.). New York: Disney-Hyperion Books.

Hicks, D. (2017–2021). *The lost art mysteries* series. New York: Clarion Books.

Hiebert, E. H. (2017). The texts of literacy instruction: Obstacles to or opportunities for educational equity? *Literacy Research: Theory, Method, and Practice, 66*(1), 117–134.

Hiebert, E. H. (2019). *Teaching words and how they work: Small changes for big vocabulary results*. New York: Teachers College Press.

Hill, L. C. (2013). *When the beat was born: DJ Kool Herc and the creation of hip hop* (T. Taylor, Illus.). New York: Roaring Brook Press.

Hinton, S. E. (1967). *The outsiders*. New York: Penguin.

Hintz, A., & Smith, A. T. (2021). *Mathematizing children's literature: Sparking connections, joy, and wonder through read-alouds and discussion*. Portsmouth, NH: Stenhouse.

Hirasuna, D. (2005). *The art of Gaman: Arts and crafts form the Japanese American internment camps, 1942–1946*. New York: Ten Speed Press.

Hodge, S. (2017). *Artists and their pets: True stories of famous artists and their animal friends* (V. Lemay, Illus.). New York: Duo Press.

Hoffman, J. L., Teale, W. H., & Yokota, J. (2015). *The book matters! Choosing complex narrative texts to support literary discussion*. Accessed at https://naeyc.org/resources/pubs/yc/sep2015/book-matters on February 1, 2023.

Holub, J. (2016). *What was Woodstock?* (G. Copeland, Illus.). New York: Grosset & Dunlap.

Horowitz-Kraus, T., Vannest, J. J., & Holland, S. K. (2013). Overlapping neural circuitry for narrative comprehension and proficient reading in children and adolescents. *Neuropsychologia, 51*(13), 2651–2662.

Hughes, K. (2020). *Displacement*. New York: First Second.

Hung, P., Hwang, G., Lee, Y., Wu, T., Vogel, B., Milrad, M., et al. (2014). A problem-based ubiquitous learning approach to improving the questioning abilities of elementary school students. *Educational Technology and Society, 17*(4), 316–334.

Hurst, S., & Griffity, P. (2015). Examining the effect of teacher read-aloud on adolescent attitudes and learning. *Middle Grade Research Journal, 10*(1), 31–47.

Hutton, J. S., Phelan, K., Horowitz-Kraus, T., Dudley, J., Altaye, M., DeWitt, T., et al. (2017). Story time turbocharger? Child engagement during shared reading and cerebellar activation and connectivity in preschool-age children listening to stories. *PLOS ONE, 12*(5).

Håland, A., Hoem, T. F., & McTigue, E. M. (2021). The quantity and quality of teachers' self-perceptions of read-aloud practices in Norwegian first grade classrooms. *Early Childhood Education Journal, 49*(1), 1–14. Accessed at https://doi.org/10.1007/s10643-020-01053-5 on July 14, 2023.

Ignotofsky, R. (2017). *Women in sports: 50 fearless athletes who played to win.* New York: Ten Speed Press.

Ignotofsky, R. (2019). *Women in art: 50 fearless creatives who inspired the world.* New York: Ten Speed Press.

International Literacy Association. (n.d.). *Literacy glossary.* Accessed at https://www.literacyworldwide.org/get-resources/literacy-glossaryon September 16, 2022.

Ippolito, J., Dobbs, C. L., & Charner-Laird, M. (2017). What literacy means in the math class: Teacher team explores ways to remake instruction to develop students' skills. *Learning Professional, 38*(2), 66–70.

Ivey, G., & Broaddus, K. (2001). "Just plain reading": A survey of what makes students want to read in middle school classrooms. *Reading Research Quarterly, 36*(4), 350–377.

Izen, M., & West, J. (2004). *The dog who sang at the opera* (E. Oller, Illus.). New York: Abrams.

Jackson, S. (2021). *Black artists shaping the world.* London: Thames & Hudson.

Joven, C. C. (2017). *Sports Illustrated Kids: Starting line readers* series (E. Shems, & A. López, Illus.). North Mankato, MN: Stone Arch Books.

Justice, L. M., & Ezell, H. K. (2004). Print referencing: An emergent literacy enhancement strategy and its clinical applications. *Language, Speech, and Hearing Services in Schools, 35*(2), 185–193.

Justice, L. M., Pullen, P. C., & Pence, K. (2008). Influence of verbal and nonverbal references to print on preschoolers' visual attention to print during storybook reading. *Developmental Psychology, 44*(3), 855–866.

Justice, L. M., Skibbe, L., Canning, A., & Lankford, C. (2005). Pre-schoolers, print, and storybooks: An observational study using eye movement analysis. *Journal of Research in Reading, 28*(3), 229–243.

Karakus, F. (2013). A cross-age study of students' understanding of fractals. *Bolema, 27*(47), 829–846.

Kato, J. E. (2012). *Manuel's murals* (R. Smith, Illus.). Sacramento, CA: 3L.

Katstaller, R. (2022). *Skater cielo (sky).* New York: Orchard Books.

Katz, S. B., Jablonski, C., Trusiani, L., Platt, C., Leslie, T., Deutsch, S., et al. (2020–2023). *The story of: A biography series for new readers.* Emeryville, CA: Rockridge Press.

Kay, A. (2020). *Kay's anatomy: A complete (and completely disgusting) guide to the human body* (H. Parker, Illus.). New York: Delacorte Press.

Keating, J. (2016). *Pink is for blobfish: Discovering the world's perfectly pink animals* (D. DeGrand, Illus.). New York: Knopf.

Keating, J. (2019). *Gross as a snot otter: Discovering the world's most disgusting animals* (D. DeGrand, Illus.). New York: Knopf.

Keating, J. (2021). *Big as a giant snail: Discovering the world's most gigantic animals* (D. DeGrand, Illus.). New York: Knopf.

Kelly, E. E. (2015). *Blackbird fly.* New York: Greenwillow Books.

Khan, K. S., Purtell, K. M., Logan, J., Ansari, A., & Justice, L. M. (2017). Association between television viewing and parent-child reading in the early home environment. *Journal of Developmental and Behavioral Pediatrics, 38*(7), 521–527.

Kim, J. S., Rich, P., & Scherer, E. (2022, July). *Long-term effects of a sustained content literacy intervention on third graders' reading comprehension outcomes* (Ed Working Paper: 22–600). Accessed at https://edworkingpapers.com/ai22-600 on May 2, 2023.

Kleckner, S. (2021). *The art of running away.* Mendota Heights, MN: Jolly Fish Press.

Konigsburg, E. L. (2019). *From the mixed-up files of Mrs. Basil E. Frankweiler*. New York: Atheneum Books for Young Readers.

Kymes, A. (2005). Teaching online comprehension strategies using think-alouds. *Journal of Adolescent and Adult Literacy, 48*(6), 492–500.

LaBarge, M. (2020). *Women artists A to Z* (C. Corrigan, Illus.). New York: Dial Books for Young Readers.

Lapin, J. (2019). *If you had your birthday party on the moon* (S. Ceccarelli, Illus.). New York: Sterling Children's Books.

Lapp, D., Fisher, D., & Grant, M. (2008). "You can read this text—I'll show you how": Interactive comprehension instruction. *Journal of Adolescent and Adult Literacy, 51*(5), 372–383.

Larson, H. (2018). *All summer long*. New York: Farrar, Straus & Giroux.

Layne, S. L. (2015). *In defense of read-aloud: Sustaining best practice*. Portland, ME: Stenhouse.

Ledger, S., & Merga, M. K. (2018). Reading aloud: Children's attitudes toward being read to at home and at school. *Australian Journal of Teacher Education, 43*(3). http://dx.doi.org/10.14221/ajte.2018v43n3.8

Lee, H. (1960). *To kill a mockingbird*. Philadelphia: Lippincott.

Lee-Tai, A. (2006). *A place where sunflowers grow* (F. Hoshino, Illus.). New York: Children's Book Press.

Legare, C. H., Mills, C. M., Souza, A. L., Plummer, L. E., & Yasskin, R. (2013). The use of questions as problem-solving strategies during early childhood. *Journal of Experimental Child Psychology, 114*(1), 63–76.

Lennon, J. (2017). *Imagine* (J. Jillien, Illus.). London: Lincoln's Childrens Books.

Lennon, J., & McCartney, P. (2019). *All you need is love* (M. Rosenthal, Illus.). New York: Little Simon.

Lennox, S. (2013). Interactive read-alouds—An avenue for enhancing children's language for thinking and understanding: A review of recent research. *Early Childhood Education Journal, 41*(5), 381–389.

Levin, T. (1981). *Effective instruction*. Alexandria, VA: ASCD.

Levinson, C. (2021). *The people's painter: How Ben Shahn fought for justice with art* (E. Turk, Illus.). New York: Abrams Books for Young Readers.

Linder, D. E., Mueller, M. K., Gibbs, D. M., Alper, J. A., & Freeman, L. M. (2018). Effects of an animal-assisted intervention on reading skills and attitudes in second grade students. *Early Childhood Education Journal, 46*(3), 323–329.

Lithgow, J. (2013). *Never play music right next to the zoo* (L. Hernandez, Illus.). New York: Simon & Schuster Books for Young Readers.

Littlejohn, J. (2018). *B is for baller: The ultimate basketball alphabet* (M. Shipley, Illus.). Chicago: Triumph Books.

Littlejohn, J. (2019). *G is for golazo: The ultimate soccer alphabet* (M. Shipley, Illus.). Chicago: Triumph Books.

Logan, J. A. R., Justice, L. M., Yumuş, M., & Chaparro-Moreno, L. J. (2019). When children are not read to at home: The million word gap. *Journal of Developmental and Behavioral Pediatrics, 40*(5), 383–386.

Love, M. (2016). *Good vibrations: My life as a Beach Boy*. New York: Blue Rider Press.

Love, M., & Wilson, B. (2020). *Good vibrations* (P. Hoppe, Illus.). New York: Akashic Books.

Lovedahl, A. N., & Bricker, P. (2006). Using biographies in science class. *Science and Children, 44*(3), 38–43.

Lovelace, S., & Stewart, S. R. (2007). Increasing print awareness in preschoolers with language impairment using non-evocative print referencing. *Language, Speech, and Hearing Services in Schools, 38*(1), 16–30.

MacKnight, W. M. (2018). *The frame-up*. New York: Greenwillow Books.

Mandelbrot, B. (2010). *Fractals and the art of roughness* [Video file]. Accessed at https://www.ted.com/talks/benoit_mandelbrot_fractals_and_the_art_of_roughness?language=en on February 6, 2023.

Marchessault, J. K., & Larwin, K. H. (2014). The potential impact of structured read-aloud on middle school reading achievement. *International Journal of Evaluation and Research in Education, 3*(3), 187–196.

Marley, C. (2019). *Get up, stand up* (J. J. Cabuay, Illus.). San Francisco: Chronicle Books.

Martin, B., Jr. (1970). *Brown bear, brown bear, what do you see?* (E. Carle, Illus.). New York: Holt, Rinehart & Winston.

Maughan, S. (2023). The audiobook market, and its revenue, keep growing. *Publishers Weekly*. Acessed at https://www.publishersweekly.com/pw/by-topic/industry-news/audio-books/article/92444-the-audiobook-market-and-revenue-keeps-growing.html on July 26, 2023

May, L. (2011). Animating talk and texts: Culturally relevant teacher read-alouds of informational texts. *Journal of Literacy Research, 43*(1), 3–38.

Mazeika, K. (2022). *Annette feels free: The true story of Annette Kellerman, world-class swimmer, fashion pioneer, and real-life mermaid*. New York: Beach Lane Books.

McCaffrey, M., & Hisrich, K. E. (2017). Read-alouds in the classroom: A pilot study of teachers' self-reporting practices. *Reading Improvement, 54*(3), 93–100.

McClure, E. L., & Fullerton, S. K. (2017). Instructional interactions: Supporting students' reading development through interactive read-alouds of informational texts. *The Reading Teacher, 71*(1), 51–59.

McCulley, L., Swanson, E., Wanzek, J., Vaughn, S., Stillman, S., Hairrell, A., et al. (2012). *Text reading in secondary English language arts and social studies classes: An observation study* [Poster presentation]. Pacific Coast Research Conference, San Diego, CA.

McGeown, S., Bonsall, J., Andries, V., Howarth, D., & Wilkinson, K. (2020). Understanding reading motivation across different text types: Qualitative insights from children. *Journal of Research in Reading, 43*(4), 597–608.

McKeown, R.G., & Gentilucci, J. L. (2007). Think-aloud strategy: Metacognitive development and monitoring comprehension in the middle school second-language classroom. *Journal of Adolescent and Adult Literacy, 51*(2), 136–147.

McTigue, E., Douglass, A., Wright, K. L., Hodges, T. S., & Franks, A. D. (2015). Beyond the story map. *The Reading Teacher, 69*(1), 91–101.

Meltzer, B. (2014–2023). *Ordinary people change the world* (C. Eliopoulos, Illus.). New York: Penguin.

Mendelsohn, A. L., & Klass, P. (2018). Early language exposure and middle school language and IQ: Implications for primary prevention. *Pediatrics, 142*(4). Accessed at https://doi.org/10.1542/peds.2018-2234 on July 14, 2023.

Merga, M. K., & Ledger, S. (2019). Teachers' attitudes toward and frequency of engagement in reading aloud in the primary classroom. *Literacy, 53*(3), 134–142.

Mesmer, H. A. E. (2016). Text matters: Exploring the lexical reservoirs of books in preschool rooms. *Early Childhood Research Quarterly, 34*, 67–77.

Miranda, A. (2019). *Tangled: A story about shapes* (E. Comstock, Illus.). New York: Simon & Schuster Books for Young Readers.

Miyakoshi, A. (2019). *The piano recital*. Toronto, Ontario, Canada: Kids Can Press.

Mochizuki, K. (1993). *Baseball saved us* (D. Lee, Illus.). New York: Lee & Low Books.

Mol, S. E., & Bus, A. G. (2011). To read or not to read: A meta-analysis of print exposure from infancy to early adulthood. *Psychological Bulletin, 137*(2), 267–296.

Moll, L. C., Amanti, C., Neff, D., & Gonzalez, N. (1992). Funds of knowledge for teaching: Using a qualitative approach to connect homes and classrooms. *Theory Into Practice, 31*(2), 132–141.

Montag, J. L., Jones, M. N., & Smith, L. B. (2015). The words children hear: Picture books and the statistics for language learning. *Psychological Science, 26*(9), 1489–1496.

Morland, C. (2020). *Music and how it works: The complete guide for kids* (D. Humphries, Illus.). New York: Dorling Kindersley (DK).

Morton, B. A., & Dalton, B. (2007). *Changes in instructional hours in four subjects by public school teachers of grades 1 through 4.* Washington, DC: National Center for Education Statistics.

Mosca, J. F. (2017). *The girl who thought in pictures: The story of Dr. Temple Grandin* (D. Rieley, Illus.). Seattle, WA: Innovation Press.

Mosca, J. F. (2018). *The girl with a mind for math: The story of Raye Montague* (D. Rieley, Illus.). Seattle, WA: Innovation Press.

Moschovaki, E., & Meadows, S. (2005). Young children's cognitive engagement during classroom book reading: Differences according to book, text genre, and story format. *Early Childhood Research and Practice, 7*(2), 51–65.

Moss, L. (2005). *Zin! Zin! Zin! A violin* (M. Priceman, Illus.). New York: Aladdin.

Moss, M. (2013). *Barbed wire baseball: How one man brought hope to the Japanese internment camps of WWII* (Y. Shimizu, Illus.). New York: Abrams Books for Young Readers.

Moussa, W., Koester, E., & Alonge, O. (2018). *Effectiveness of read-aloud instruction on reading and math outcomes: Evidence from Northern Nigeria.* Washington, DC: Education Policy and Data Center.

Moyer J. E. (2011). What does it really mean to "read" a text? *Journal of Adolescent and Adult Literacy, 55*(3), 253–256.

Mulford, Z. (2019). *The president sang Amazing Grace* (J. Scher, Illus.). Petaluma, CA: Cameron Kids.

Murphy, P. (2009) Using picture books to engage middle school students. *Middle School Journal, 40*(4), 20–24.

Nabais, R. (2019). *The history of rock: For big fans and little punks* (J. Raimundo, Illus.). Chicago: Triumph Books.

Napier, M. (2002). *Z is for Zamboni: A hockey alphabet* (M. Rose, Illus.). Chelsea, MI: Sleeping Bear Press.

National Council for the Social Studies. (2010). *National curriculum standards for social studies: A framework for teaching, learning, and assessment.* Silver Spring, MD: Author.

National Geographic Kids. (2016). *Weird but true! Sports: 300 wacky facts about awesome athletics.* Washington, DC: National Geographic.

National Literacy Trust. (2013). *A guide to text types: Narrative, non-fiction and poetry.* Accessed at https://thomastallisschool.com/uploads/2/2/8/7/2287089/guide_to_text_types_final-1.pdf on February 1, 2023.

National Public Media. (2022). *The spoken word audio report.* Accessed https://www.nationalpublicmedia.com/insights/reports/the-spoken-word-audio-report/ on February 1, 2023.

Ness, M. (2009). Reading comprehension strategies in secondary content area classrooms: Teacher use of and attitudes towards reading comprehension instruction. *Reading Horizons, 49*(2), 143–166.

Ness, M. (2011). Explicit reading comprehension instruction in elementary classrooms: Teacher use of reading comprehension strategies. *Journal of Research in Childhood Education, 25*(1), 98–117.

Ness, M. (2014). Moving students' questions out of the parking lot. *The Reading Teacher, 67*(5), 369–373.

Ness, M. (2016). When readers ask questions: Inquiry-based reading instruction. *The Reading Teacher*, *70*(2), 189–196.

Ness, M. (2018). *Think big with think alouds, grades K–5: A three-step planning process that develops strategic readers.* Thousand Oaks, CA: Corwin Press.

Ness, M. (2019b). When students generate questions: Participatory-based reading instruction in elementary classrooms. In A. Eckhoff (Ed.), *Participatory research with young children* (pp. 73–87). Cham, Switzerland: Springer.

Ness, M. (Host). (2019a). What is a book desert? [Audio podcast]. In *End Book Deserts*. Accessed at www.endbookdeserts.com/podcast on February 3, 2023.

Neuman, S. B., & Moland, N. (2019). Book deserts: The consequences of income segregation on children's access to print. *Urban Education*, *54*(1), 126–147.

Neuschwander, C., Einhorn, E., Kroll, V., & Sparagna LoPresti, A. (1997–2014). *Charlesbridge math adventures* (W. Geehan, D. Clark, P. O'Neill, & P. Hornung, Illus.). Watertown, MA: Charlesbridge.

NGSS Lead States. (2013). *Next Generation Science Standards: For states, by states.* Washington, DC: The National Academies Press.

Nichols, D. (2021). *Art of protest: Creating, discovering, and activating art for your revolution* (D. Dagadita, S. Saddo, O. Twist, M. Mendoza, & D. Becas, Illus.). Somerville, MA: Candlewick Press.

Ortlieb, E., & Norris, M. (2012). Using the think-aloud strategy to bolster reading comprehension of science concepts. *Current Issues in Education*, *15*(1), 1–10.

O'Connor, R. E., Bocian, K., Beebe-Frankenberger, M., & Linklater, D. L. (2010). Responsiveness of students with language difficulties to early intervention in reading. *The Journal of Special Education*, *43*(4), 220–235.

Parker-Pope, T. (2022, March 28). Broken butts and questioning cats: Bring on subversive books for kids. *The New York Times*. Accessed at https://nytimes.com/2022/03/24/well/kids-books-subversive.html on May 8, 2023.

Paul, R. (2011). *Stomp!* New York: Scholastic

Paulsen, G. (1999). *Hatchet.* New York: Aladdin.

Pearson, P. D., & Gallagher, M. C. (1983). The instruction of reading comprehension. *Contemporary Educational Psychology*, *8*(3), 317–344.

Pellum, K. B. (2019). *Black women in science: A Black history book for kids* (K. Morris, Illus.). Emeryville, CA: Rockridge Press.

Perry, S., Mattern, J., & Ventura, M. (2020). *No barriers* series. Hopkins, MN: 12-Story Library.

Peterson, D. S., & Taylor, B. M. (2012). Using higher order questioning to accelerate students' growth in reading. *The Reading Teacher*, *65*(5), 295–304.

Pinkney, A. D. (2021). *Harriet Tubman* (G. Flint, Illus.). New York: Philomel Books.

Pratt, S. & Hodges, T. (2022). The think-aloud observation protocol: Developing a literacy instruction tool for teacher reflection and growth. *Reading Psychology*, *44*(1), 1–31.

Pressley, G. M. (1976). Mental imagery helps eight-year-olds remember what they read. *Journal of Educational Psychology*, *68*(3), 355–359.

Price, L. H., van Kleeck, A., & Huberty, C. J. (2009). Talk during book sharing between parents and preschool children: A comparison between storybook and expository book conditions. *Reading Research Quarterly*, *44*(2), 171–194.

Rajan, R. S. (2022). *The read aloud factor: How to create the habit that boosts your baby's brain.* Chicago: Parenting Press.

Rebel Girls. (2021). *Rebel Girls champions: 25 tales of unstoppable athletes.* Larkspur, CA: Author.

Recht, D. R., & Leslie, L. (1988). Effect of prior knowledge on good and poor readers' memory of text. *Journal of Educational Psychology, 80*(1), 16–20.

Redding, O. (2020). *Respect* (R. Moss, Illus.). New York: Akashic Books.

Reid, M. (2021). *Maryam's magic: The story of mathematician Maryam Mirzakhani* (A. Jaleel, Illus.). New York: Balzer and Bray.

Reynolds, P. H. (2012). *Creatrilogy*. Somerville, MA: Candlewick Press.

Reynoso, N. (2021). *Courageous history makers: 11 women from Latin America who changed the world* (J. Leal, Illus.). Los Angeles: Con Todo Press.

Rhee, H. K. (2020). *The paper kingdom* (P. Campion, Illus.). New York: Random House.

Richards, M., & Schweitzer, D. (2021). *A history of music for children* (R. Blake, Illus.). New York: Thames & Hudson.

Riley, S. (2021). *The floating field: How a group of Thai boys built their own soccer field* (N. Quang, & K. Lien, Illus.). Minneapolis, MN: Millbrook Press.

Robeson, T. (2019). *Queen of physics: How Wu Chien Shiung helped unlock the secrets of the atom* (R. Huang, Illus.). New York: Sterling.

Robinson, A. (2021). A comparison between preschool teachers' read-aloud techniques with fictional and informational picture books in small groups. *Reading Horizons, 60*(1), 72–94.

Rocco, J. (2020). *How we got to the moon: The people, technology, and daring feats of science behind humanity's greatest adventure*. New York: Crown Books for Young Readers.

Rosenshine, B. V. (2015). How time is spent in elementary classrooms. *Journal of Classroom Interaction, 50*(1), 41–53.

Rosenstock, B. (2017). *Vincent can't sleep: Van Gogh paints the night sky* (M. GrandPré, Illus.). New York: Knopf.

Ross, R. L. (2017). *Exploring teachers' read-aloud book selections: What drives the decision* [Doctoral dissertation, Clemson University]. Tiger Prints. Accessed at https://tigerprints.clemson.edu/all _dissertations/2049 on July 14, 2023.

Rowling, J. K. (1998). *Harry Potter and the Sorcerer's Stone*. New York: Scholastic.

Russell-Brown, K. (2020). *She was the first! The trailblazing life of Shirley Chisholm* (E. Velasquez, Illus.). New York: Lee & Low Books.

Ryan, P. M. (1999). *Amelia and Eleanor go for a ride* (B. Selznick, Illus.). New York: Scholastic Press.

Ryan, P. M. (2002). *When Marian sang: The true recital of Marian Anderson* (B. Selznick, Illus.). New York: Scholastic Press.

Sachar, L. (2001). *Holes*. New York: Dell Laurel-Leaf Books.

Sadoski, M., & Paivio, A. (2004). A dual coding theoretical model of reading. In R. B. Ruddell & N. J. Unrau (Eds.), *Theoretical models and processes of reading* (5th ed., pp. 1329–1362). Newark, DE: International Reading Association.

Sadoski, M., & Paivio, A. (2007). Toward a unified theory of reading. *Scientific Studies of Reading, 11*(4), 337–356.

Saltzberg, B. (2010). *Beautiful oops!* New York: Workman.

Sanchez, R. (2015). *Spotlight soccer* (I. Waryanto, Illus.). North Mankato, MN: Stone Arch Books.

Santoro, L. E., Baker, S. K., Fien, H., Smith, J. L. M., & Chard, D. J. (2016). Using read-alouds to help struggling readers access and comprehend complex, informational text. *Teaching Exceptional Children, 48*(6), 282–292.

Scarborough, H. S. (2001). Connecting early language and literacy to later reading (dis)abilities: Evidence, theory, and practice. In S. B. Neuman & D. K. Dickinson (Eds.), *Handbook of early literacy research* (pp. 97–110). New York: Guilford Press.

Scholastic. (n.d.). *Teacher & principal school report.* Accessed at https://www.scholastic.com/site/teacher-principal-school-report.html on September 16, 2022.

Schrodt, K., Fain, J. G., & Hasty, M. (2015). Exploring culturally relevant texts with kindergartners and their families. *The Reading Teacher, 68*(8), 589–598.

Scott, C. M., & Balthazar, C. (2013). The role of complex sentence knowledge in children with reading and writing difficulties. *Perspectives on Language and Literacy, 39*(3), 18–30.

Scott, J., Spangler, B., & Sweet, M. (2021). *Unbound: The life + art of Judith Scott* (M. Sweet, Illus.). New York: Knopf.

Sewall, G. T. (1988). American history textbooks: Where do we go from here? *Phi Delta Kappan, 69*(8), 552–558.

Shanahan, T. (2021, September 11). *Do you see visualization as an effective reading comprehension strategy? And, for whom?* [Blog post]. Accessed at https://www.shanahanonliteracy.com/blog/do-you-see-visualization-as-an-effective-reading-comprehension-strategy-and-for-whom on February 1, 2023.

Shanahan, T. (2022, November 12). *Shared reading in the structured literacy era* [Blog post]. Accessed at www.shanahanonliteracy.com/blog/shared-reading-in-the-structured-literacy-era on February 1, 2023.

Sheridan-Thomas, H. K. (2014). Assisting struggling readers with textbook comprehension. In K. A. Hinchman & H. K. Sheridan-Thomas (Eds.), *Best practices in adolescent literacy instruction* (2nd ed., pp. 266–287). New York: Guilford Press.

Shetterly, M. L. (2018). *Hidden figures: The true story of four black women and the space race* (L. Freeman, Illus.). New York: Harper.

Siddiqui, M. (2021). *Barakah beats.* New York: Scholastic.

Singh, M. (2014, October 27). *What's going on inside the brain of a curious child?* Accessed at https://www.kqed.org/mindshift/38260/whats-going-on-inside-the-brain-of-a-curious-child on February 1, 2023.

Singh, S. J. (2020). *Fauja Singh keeps going: The true story of the oldest person to ever run a marathon* (B. Kaur, Illus.). New York: Kokila.

Sipe, L. R. (2008). *Storytime: Young children's literary understanding in the classroom.* New York: Teachers College Press.

Smith, K. C., & Hiebert, E. H. (2022, May 2). *What does research say about the texts we use in elementary school?* Accessed at https://kappanonline.org/research-texts-elementary-school-conradi-smith-hiebert on February 1, 2023.

Smith, K. C., Young, C. A., & Yatzeck, J. C. (2022). What are teachers reading and why? An analysis of elementary read aloud titles and the rationales underlying teachers' selections. *Literacy Research and Instruction, 61*(4), 383–401.

Snow, C. (2000). *Reading for understanding: Towards and R&D program in reading comprehension.* Washington, DC: RAND Corporation.

Solis, N. (2021). *The color collector* (R. Metallinou, Illus.). Ann Arbor, MI: Sleeping Bear Press.

Stabler, D. (2016). *Kid artists: True tales of childhood from creative legends* (D. Horner, Illus.). Philadelphia: Quirk Books.

Stark-McGinnis, S. (2020). *The space between lost and found.* New York: Bloomsbury.

Steig, W. (1986). *Brave Irene.* New York: Farrar, Straus & Giroux.

Steig, W. (1998). *Pete's a pizza.* New York: HarperCollins.

Stevens, C. (2021). *Peace train* (P. H. Reynolds, Illus.). New York: Harper.

Stocker, S. (2022). *Listen: How Evelyn Glennie, a deaf girl, changed percussion* (S. Holzwarth, Illus.). New York: Dial Books.

Strachan, S. L. (2015). Kindergarten students' social studies and content literacy learning from interactive read-alouds. *The Journal of Social Studies Research, 39*(4), 207–223.

Stroker, A., & Davidowitz, S. (2021). *The chance to fly.* New York: Amulet Books.

Stuart, C. (2019). *The language of the universe: A visual exploration of mathematics* (X. Abadía, Illus.). Somerville, MA: Big Picture Press.

Sullivan, S. (2011). *Passing the music down* (B. Root, Illus.). Somerville, MA: Candlewick Press.

Sun, C. (2020). Using interactive picture-book read-alouds with middle school EFL students. *English Language Teaching, 13*(7), 130–139.

Swanson, E., Wanzek, J., Petscher, Y., Vaughn. S., Heckert, J., Cavanaugh, C., et al. (2011). A synthesis of read-aloud interventions on early reading outcomes among preschool through third graders at risk for reading difficulties. *Journal of Learning Disabilities, 44*(3), 258–275.

Taboada, A., & Guthrie, J. T. (2006). Contributions of student questioning and prior knowledge to construction of knowledge from reading information text. *Journal of Literacy Research, 38*(1), 1–35.

Taie, S., & Goldring, R. (2020). *Characteristics of public and private elementary and secondary school teachers in the United States: Results from the 2017–18 national teacher and principal survey first look.* Washington, DC: National Center for Education Statistics. Accessed at https://nces.ed.gov /pubs2020/2020142.pdf on February 1, 2023.

Takei, G., Eisinger, J., & Scott, S. (2020). *They called us enemy* (H. Becker, Illus.). San Diego, California: Top Shelf.

Tang, G. (2001). *The grapes of math: Mind stretching math riddles* (H. Briggs, Illus.). New York: Scholastic.

Therrien, W. J., & Hughes, C. (2008). Comparison of repeated reading and question generation on students' reading fluency and comprehension. *Learning Disabilities, 6*(1), 1–16.

Thimmesh, C. (2018). *Girls think of everything: Stories of ingenious inventions by women* (M. Sweet, Illus.). Boston: Houghton Mifflin.

Thimmesh, C. (2022). *Girls solve everything: Stories of women entrepreneurs building a better world* (M. Sweet, Illus.). Boston: Houghton Mifflin.

Thomas, A. (2017). *The hate u give.* New York: Balzer and Bray.

Thompson, E., & Melchior, S. (2020). Improving empathy in children: Interactive read-aloud as a counseling intervention. *Journal of Creativity in Mental Health, 15*(2), 199–211.

Thompson, L. A. (2015). *Emmanuel's dream: The true story of Emmanuel Ofosu Yeboah* (S. Qualls, Illus.). New York: Schwartz & Wade Books.

Todd, T. N. (2021). *Nina: A story of Nina Simone* (C. Robinson, Illus.). New York: Putnam's.

Todd, T. N. (2022). *Holding her own: The exceptional life of Jackie Ormes* (S. Wright, Illus.). New York: Orchard Books.

Tokuda-Hall, M. (2022). *Love in the library* (Y. Imamura, Illus.). Somerville, MA: Candlewick Press.

Torres, J. (2021). *Stealing home* (D. Namisato, Illus.). Toronto, Ontario, Canada: Kids Can Press.

Towson, J. A., Akemoglu, Y., Watkins, L., & Zeng, S. (2021). Shared interactive book reading interventions for young children with disabilities: A systematic review. *American Journal of Speech-Language Pathology, 30*(6), 2700–2715.

Trelease, J. (1989). *The new read-aloud handbook.* New York: Penguin Books.

Trube, B. (2018). *Math coloring book: Fractals.* East Montpelier, VT: Green Frog.

Trusty, K. (2021). *Black inventors: 15 inventions that changed the world* (J. Polk, Illus.). Emeryville, CA: Rockridge Press.

Tullet, H. (2014). *Mix it up!* San Francisco: Handprint Books.

van den Heuvel-Panhuizen, M., & Elia, I. (2012). Developing a framework for the evaluation of picturebooks that support kindergartners' learning of mathematics. *Research in Mathematics Education, 14*(1), 17–47.

van den Heuvel-Panhuizen, M., Elia, I., & Robitzsch, A. (2016). Effects of reading picture books on kindergartners' mathematics performance. *Educational Psychology, 36*(2), 323–346.

Van Dusen, C. (2009). *The circus ship.* Somerville, MA: Candlewick Press.

Venable, C. A. F. (2020). *The oboe goes boom boom boom* (L. Cho, Illus.). New York: Greenwillow Books.

Verde, S. (2018). *Hey, wall: A story of art and community* (J. Parra, Illus.). New York: Simon & Schuster Books for Young Readers.

Verden, C. E. (2012). Reading culturally relevant literature aloud to urban youths with behavioral challenges. *Journal of Adolescent and Adult Literacy, 55*(7), 619–628.

Vere, E. (2023). *The artist.* New York: Doubleday for Young Readers.

Vergara, M. I. S. (2016–2023). *Little people, big dreams series.* London: Frances Lincoln Children's Books.

Vlach, S. K., Lentz, T. S., & Muhammad, G. F. (2023). Activating joy through culturally and historically responsive read-alouds. *The Reading Teacher.* Accessed at https://ila.onlinelibrary.wiley.com/doi/full/10.1002/trtr.2203 on April 28, 2023.

Wade, J. (2021). *Nano: The spectacular science of the very (very) small* (M. Castrillón, Illus.). Somerville, MA: Candlewick Press.

Wakefield, J. F. (2006, April 21). *Textbook usage in the United States: The case of U.S. history.* Paper presented at the International Seminar on Textbooks, Santiago, Chile.

Wallmark, L. (2017). *Grace Hopper: Queen of computer code* (K. Wu, Illus.). New York: Sterling Children's Books.

Walther, M. (2019). *The ramped-up read aloud: What to notice as you turn the page.* Thousand Oaks, CA: Corwin Literacy.

Wang, A. (2021). *Watercress* (J. Chin, Illus.). New York: Porter Books.

Wargin, K. (2004). *M is for melody: A music alphabet* (K. Larson, Illus.). Chelsea, MI: Sleeping Bear Press.

Warhola, J. (2003). *Uncle Andy's: A faabbbulous visit with Andy Warhol.* New York: Putnam's.

Wasik, B. A., & Bond, M. (2001). Beyond the pages of a book: Interactive book reading and language development in preschool classrooms. *Journal of Educational Psychology, 93*(2), 243–250.

Wasik, B. A., Hindman, A. H., & Snell, E. K. (2016). Book reading and vocabulary development: A systematic review. *Early Childhood Research Quarterly, 37*(4), 39–57.

Weatherford, C. B. (2019). *The roots of rap: 16 bars on the 4 pillars of hip-hop* (F. Morrison, Illus.). New York: Little Bee Books.

Weiss, B. (2018). *Fractals: A world in a grain of sand* [Video file]. Accessed at https://www.ted.com/talks/ben_weiss_fractals_a_world_in_a_grain_of_sand/up-next on February 6, 2023.

Wells, M. (2014). *Eddie Red undercover: Mystery on Museum Mile* (M. Calo, Illus.). Boston: Houghton Mifflin Harcourt.

Weltman, A. (2021). *The book of math: Adventures in the world of shapes and numbers* (P. Boston, Illus.). Tulsa, OK: Kane Miller Books.

Westbrook, J., Sutherland, J., Oakhill, J., & Sullivan, S. (2019). "Just reading": The impact of a faster pace of reading narratives on the comprehension of poorer adolescent readers in English classrooms. *Literacy, 53*(2), 60–68.

Wexler, N. (2019). *The knowledge gap: The hidden cause of America's broken education system—and how to fix it*. New York: Avery.

What Works Clearinghouse. (2010). *Dialogic reading: What Works Clearinghouse intervention report*. Washington, DC: Author. Accessed at https://files.eric.ed.gov/fulltext/ED509373.pdf on February 2, 2023.

Wherry (2004). The influence of home on school success. *Principal*. Accessed at https://www.naesp.org /sites/default/files/resources/2/Principal/2004/S-Op6.pdf on July 26, 2023.

White, E. B. (1952). *Charlotte's web* (G. Williams, Illus.). New York: Harper.

Whitehurst, G. J., Arnold, D. S., Epstein, J. N., Angell, A. L, Smith, M., & Fischel, J. E. (1994). A picture book reading intervention in day care and home for children from low-income families. *Developmental Psychology, 30*(5), 679-689.

Whitehurst, G. J., Fischel, J. E., Arnold, D., Lonigan, C., Valdez-Menchaca, M., & Caulfield, M. (1989). Intervening in early shared book reading: Scripts vs. direct training. *Society for Research in Child Development (SRCD) Abstracts, 7*, 94.

Willems, M. (2004). *Knuffle bunny: A cautionary tale*. New York: Hyperion Books for Children.

Willems, M. (2019). *Because* (A. Ren, Illus.). New York: Hyperion Books for Children.

Williams, A. D. (2021). *Shirley Chisholm dared: The story of the first Black woman in Congress* (A. Harrison, Illus.). New York: Schwartz Books.

Willingham, D. (2012, March 7). *School time, knowledge, and reading comprehension* [Blog post]. Accessed at http://www.danielwillingham.com/daniel-willingham-science-and-education-blog/school -time-knowledge-and-reading-comprehensionon May 2, 2023.

Winter, J. (2017). *The world is not a rectangle: A portrait of architect Zaha Hadid*. New York: Beach Lane Books.

Winter, J. (2019). *Elvis is king!* (Red Nose Studio, Illus.). New York: Schwartz & Wade Books.

Wiseman, A. (2011). Interactive read alouds: Teachers and students constructing knowledge and literacy together. *Early Childhood Education Journal, 38*(6), 431–438.

Wiseman, A. (2012). Resistance, engagement, and understanding: A profile of a struggling emergent reader responding to read-alouds in a kindergarten classroom. *Reading and Writing Quarterly, 28*(3), 255–278.

Woo, E. (2019). *It's a numberful world: How math is hiding everywhere*. New York: The Experiment.

Woodward, C. V. (2022). *Family dynamics: Embrace your sound* (T. Vu, Illus.). Four Hearts Books.

World of Words. (n.d.). *Powered by research*.

Wright, T. S. (2019). Reading to learn from the start: The power of interactive read-alouds. *American Educator, 42*(4), 4–8.

Wright, T. S., & Neuman, S. B. (2014). Paucity and disparity in kindergarten oral vocabulary instruction. *Journal of Literacy Research, 46*(3), 330–357.

Yamasaki, K., & Lender, I. (2020). *Everything Naomi loved* (K. Yamasaki, Illus.). New York: Norton Young Readers.

Yang, K. (2022). *Yes we will: Asian Americans who shaped this country* (N. H. Ali, F. Azim, M. Chin, S. Deng, S. Gupta, J. Kuo, et al., Illus.). New York: Dial Books for Young Readers.

Yopp, H. K., & Yopp, R. H. (2014). *Literature-based reading activities: Engaging students with literary and informational text* (6th ed.). Upper Saddle River, NJ: Pearson.

Yopp, R. H., & Yopp, H. K. (2006). Informational texts as read-alouds at school and home. *Journal of Literacy Research, 38*(1), 37–51.

Young, T. A., Monroe, E. E., & Roth-McDuffie, A. (2021). Picturebook biography read-alouds and standards for mathematical practice. *The Reading Teacher, 75*(2), 135–146.

Zucker, T. A., Justice, L. M., Piasta, S. B., & Kaderavek, J. N. (2010). Preschool teachers' literal and inferential questions and children's responses during whole-class shared reading. *Early Childhood Research Quarterly, 25*(1), 65–83.

Zucker, T. A., Ward, A. E., & Justice, L. M. (2009). Print referencing during read-alouds: A technique for increasing emergent readers' print knowledge. *The Reading Teacher, 63*(1), 62–72.

Zuckerman, G. (with Zuckerman, E., & Zuckerman, G.). (2016). *Rising above: How 11 athletes overcame challenges in their youth to become stars.* New York: Philomel Books.

Zwaan, R. A., Stanfield, R. A., & Yaxley, R. H. (2002). Language comprehenders mentally represent the shapes of objects. *Psychological Science, 13*(2), 168–171.

Zweig, B. (Writer). (2008). In Executive Producers Henson, B., Henson, L., Stanford, H., & Zweig, B., *Sid the Science Kid* [Television series]. Los Angeles: PBS Kids.

Index